PAUL AND THE GALATIANS

Paul E.
Stroble

PAUL and the GALATIANS

The Life and Letters of Paul

Abingdon Press
Nashville

PAUL AND THE GALATIANS

ISBN 0-687-09023-7

00 01 02 03 04 05 06 07 08 09 — 10 9 8 7 6 5 4 3 2 1

Manufactured in the United States of America

CONTENTS

HOW TO USE THIS RESOURCE

Welcome to *Paul and the Galatians*, a six-session study on Paul's letter and his relationship with the Galatian congregations. Each of the six chapters contains common elements designed to help you use this resource successfully in a group setting or as a personal study.

"Read Galatians"

First you will note throughout each chapter that there are a number of subheadings that direct you to read a portion of Galatians. While there may also be cross references to numerous other passages in the Bible, the Galatians passage is the key to the lesson. If this is an individual endeavor, you can read the Bible references as you encounter them.

Convenient Short Blocks of Text

Second you will find that the subheadings break up text into segments that are usually about two-to-three pages long. While the information in the chapter forms a coherent whole, the ideas are "sized" so that you can not only take the long view but also spend time with distinct ideas within the whole.

Study Questions

At the end of each of these divisions within the chapter are study and discussion questions that relate to that segment of the text. Many of the questions are designed to make sure you understand the biblical text. Galatians is a complicated piece of Scripture, and the apostle's argument may sound foreign or confusing to 21st-century culture.

Other questions are more analytical and ask readers to assess meanings for the original audience. That understanding leads to another level of study helps: personal reflection on what the revealed meaning of the biblical passage means and how those learnings and faithful insights can be applied to one's life.

Closing

At the end of each chapter are some suggestions for closing that apply to both a group and an individual setting. Many times you will be asked to summarize the content and import of that chapter and the selected Scripture. In each instance, you are invited to a time of prayer.

Leading a Group

If you are leading a group, these pointers will help you plan the study session:

• Read the entire chapter, including all the Scriptures.
• Think about your group members: their needs, their experience with the Bible and with each other, their questions. From this information, establish one or two session goals.

• Pay particular attention to the study questions and select at least one or two questions, if possible, from each segment of the text. Keeping in mind your group and your goals, note which questions you intend to cover. Try to have a variety of content, analytical, and personal application questions and activities.

• Encourage group members to use their Bibles and to read these texts.

• Be comfortable with silence and give group members a chance to think. Be sure that no one dominates and that everyone has the opportunity to participate.

• Have an intentional closure to the session by engaging in the suggested prayer or other spiritual discipline.

• Accept our best wishes and blessings for a transformational and edifying study time.

INTRODUCTION

The Letter to the Galatians is, compared to Paul's other letters, of moderate length. Compared to other New Testament writings such as the Gospels, it is short. But, as we shall see in this book, Galatians is a letter of much power and influence. Justification through faith, the power of the death and resurrection of Jesus Christ, God's love of Jew and Gentile alike, the absolute confidence we can have in salvation, the impossibility of salvation through works, the misleading quality of works, the power and evidence of the Holy Spirit, the relationship between Christ and the "old covenant": These are a few of Paul's favorite themes in many of his letters, themes that are addressed in Galatians as well.

The New Testament scholar Luke Timothy Johnson calls Galatians "the apostle at his most difficult and exhilarating." In his text *The Writings of the New Testament* (Fortress Press, 1986), Johnson writes, "Here is a brave intelligence that moves beyond an apparently narrow parochial problem to the deepest questions concerning life before God." That problem—whether Christians should be circumcised according to the Jewish covenant—becomes in Paul's letter a clarion call to Christians to embrace and live the freedom bestowed in Christ. That freedom is but one of the riches of the Christian life,

according to Paul, that can be found in the gospel message. Paul struggled, in turn, to impress that magnificent
gospel on a loving but, at the time of Paul's writing, fickle
and misled congregation.

I WHO WERE THE GALATIANS?

A Gospel Easy and Hard to Learn

The hardest to learn was the least complicated." This line from a popular song by The Indigo Girls could apply to the church at Galatia—and to us. For Paul, the gospel was not complicated. Since all have sinned, God who is rich in mercy has saved us through faith, not as the result of our own doing or because of our works, but as a completely free gift of God. More simply put: Works are nothing apart from faith, but grace working through faith is everything.

Yet this gospel is hard to learn. How many times have you felt inferior to someone who is "more spiritual" than you? How often, on the other hand, have you felt more spiritual than someone with whom you disagree? How many times have you felt superior to someone who has not passed the same spiritual "entrance requirements" as you (whether it is baptism, an Emmaus walk, a family connection, or whatever)? How many times have you offered to God in prayer the things you have done rather than counting on God's free gifts? How many times have you felt you were at the end of your rope and promised God you would do something if only God would bless you? How many times have you believed, even unconsciously, that you have to be "a good person" in order for God to love you, to bless your life and lead you to heaven?

We play these sorts of games, of course. We play them in our heads and hearts and in our relationships with each other. We substitute our works for the real thing. We look to the committees on which we have served, to the spiritual events we have attended, to the dollars we have given to the church, to the swear words we have avoided saying, and so forth and so on; and we count them as if they were currency that built up a store of personal righteousness. We look to our failures—the times we were unloving, the times we were angry and ungrateful, the times our courage failed, the times we stumbled—and believe that, somehow, God's love for us decreases each time we fall, that God withdraws from our account of salvation each time we sin.

A GOSPEL EASY AND HARD TO LEARN

• In your own spiritual journey, have you ever believed yourself less spiritual than someone else at your church? more spiritual? Have you ever "looked down your nose" at someone else? What was the result of these feelings or attitudes?
• Do you find the gospel easy, or hard, or both, to learn? Why?

God's Covenant

As ancient Scripture applicable to our daily lives, Paul's letter to the Galatians takes a stand against all that. What has God done for us? God has sent the Son to die so that we might be "justified by his grace as a gift, through the redemption that is in Christ Jesus, whom God put forward as a sacrifice of atonement by his blood, effective through faith" (Romans 3:24-25). Can we do any more than that to win God's love?

Many times in our Christian walk, we think we can. The Galatians certainly thought so. Some teachers visited the church and maintained that circumcision is necessary for Christian faith. Circumcision is, of course, the ancient rite involving the removal of the foreskin from a male's penis, a rite that was dictated by God as a sign of God's covenant with the chosen people. In ancient Hebrew religion the performance of this act was not merely a recommendation but a necessity. God told Abraham, "Every male among you shall be circumcised. . . . It shall be a sign of the covenant between me and you. Throughout your generations every male among you shall be circumcised when he is eight days old. . . . Any uncircumcised male who is not circumcised in the flesh of his foreskin shall be cut off from his people; he has broken my covenant" (Genesis 17:10-14). According to one cryptic passage, God even "tried to kill" Moses, either because he was uncircumcised or because his and Zipporah's son was uncircumcised (Exodus 4:24-26). Circumcision was a serious matter.

Circumcision is still practiced as a rite for Jewish baby boys and is also a fairly routine medical procedure for Gentile baby boys as well. Paul himself allowed Timothy to be circumcised (Acts 16:3) because Timothy was by birth a Jew (Acts 16:1-3), although Paul denied that Gentiles needed circumcision. That is Paul's point in his letter to the church in Galatia, a predominantly Gentile church. Only by faith in Christ can one be in a right relationship with God. That is, one cannot achieve a relationship with God by performing works of the law or by observing certain rites, God-given though they may be. Because of Christ, no human activity whatsoever can earn for a person a relationship with God. To think otherwise is to deny the sufficiency of God's grace (see, for instance, Galatians 2:16; 3:24-26; 6:12-15).

In Galatians we have a great statement of Christian freedom. Christ has set us free in order for us to show love to God and to one another. Although it is a short letter (less than half the length of Romans and much shorter than some of the Gospels), Galatians holds tremendous power. Writing in the *Interpretation* commentary series, Charles B. Cousar has said,

> Paul's letter to the Galatians has had an impact on the life and thought of the Christian church far exceeding its modest length. . . . During the patristic period commentaries on Galatians seem to have been more numerous than on any other of Paul's letters. The influence of the epistle on Martin Luther is well known. He found it immediately relevant to the situation of the church in the sixteenth century and wrote unquestionably the most influential commentary on the letter. . . . During the nineteenth century Galatians became the focal point of a discussion on the history of the early church, in which Paul as spokesman for Gentile Christianity was set in sharp conflict with the original apostles. . . . More recently, interpreters have found in Galatians clarification about the meaning of justification by faith, help with the identity and character of the people of God, and guidance for the responsible use of freedom. The epistle contains the strongest statement of the equality of females and males to be found in the NT (3:28).[1]

GOD'S COVENANT

• An important mark of the covenant for the ancient Jewish community was circumcision. Read Genesis 17:10-14 and Acts 16:1-3. What is the significance of this rite? What impact would or could it have in the context of a Gentile community?

• At this point in your study, why do you think it is so important for Christians to be free from the necessity of certain rites? Do you think, at this point in your study, that there are certain "entrance requirements" for Christians?

Themes in Galatians

To embark on a study of Galatians is to realize the completeness of God's love for us. The Letter to the Galatians deals with interrelated themes:

- The role of older Jewish rites such as circumcision in Christian living (especially for Gentiles)
- The broader role of the Jewish Torah, or "Law," for Christians
- The great doctrine of justification by faith
- The kind of life Christians ought to and can lead
- The source and nature of Paul's apostleship

All these themes are woven together through the greater theme of God's grace that has done everything necessary for our salvation.

THEMES IN GALATIANS

- Glance through Galatians. What are some ideas that "pop out" to you through a superficial reading? What verses seem to stand out? Keep these themes in mind throughout the course of your study.

To the Churches of Galatia
Read Galatians 1:1-5

The letter begins with Paul's customary salutation, but with perhaps a bit more edge: "Paul an apostle—sent neither by human commission nor from human authorities, but through Jesus Christ and God the Father, who raised him from the dead—and all the members of God's family who are with me,

To the churches of Galatia" (Galatians 1:1-2).

Many of Paul's letters begin in similar fashion. In his study of Paul's letters, Calvin Roetzel notes that Paul's letters follow the typical epistolary form of the time. This epistolary form is slightly different than the form to which we users of e-mail or "snail mail" are accustomed:

- Salutation, including sender, recipient, and greeting (in this case, Galatians 1:1-5)
- Thanksgiving (which is omitted in Galatians but is an important aspect of other letters, for instance, Romans 1:8-15, 1 Thessalonians 1:2-10, and so forth)
- Body (Galatians 1:6–4:31)
- Closing Commands (Galatians 5:1–6:10 and 6:11-15)
- Conclusion, including peace wish (Galatians 6:16), greetings (omitted), a kiss (omitted) and an apostolic command (6:17), and benediction (6:18).[2]

These letter-writing conventions were not considered hard and fast rules, however. According to Roetzel, Paul used these formal structures according to his own purposes, as, for instance, when he defended his apostolic authority within the salutation of Galatians. [3]

TO THE CHURCHES OF GALATIA

- Skim each of these epistolary elements and compare them to the introductory verses of others of Paul's letters (Romans through Thessalonians).
- Do these salutations give you any hints about Paul's purpose in writing and his feelings about the congregations?

Paul's Visit to Galatia

Though its subject matter is crystal clear, the letter contains some historical mysteries. For instance, who exactly were the Galatians? Gallons of scholarly ink have been spilled over the phrase "the churches of Galatia" (Galatians 1:2) in attempts to establish the identity of Paul's churches and thereby clarify the historical situation in which Paul wrote. The term *Galatia* designates two different, overlapping areas of Asia Minor (now Turkey). It is as if Paul had written "to the churches in New York," not specifying New York State or New York City or where the churches in either the state or the city were.

According to one author, the Greek and Latin words for Galatia were used interchangeably in ancient times with terms like *Galli* (Latin for Gauls) and *Celtae* or *Keltoi* (Latin and Greek, respectively, for Celts). An ancient tribe of people who originated in central Europe near the Danube River migrated into several areas. Some of these people settled in what are now Switzerland, northern Italy, and France—thus the ancient Roman name *Gaul* for the area in which they settled. Other groups of these people settled in Britain, where they became known as the Celts. Still others migrated east and invaded Asia Minor about 278 B.C. and settled in the area of Ancyra. The old Galatian region—bordered by Phrygia to the west, Paphlagonia, Bithynia, and Pontus on the north, Pontus and Cappadocia on the east, and Lycaonia on the south— lay in Asia Minor's north central section. It included the major cities of Pessinus, Ancyra, and Tavium, which were found in this region that scholars sometimes called "Old Galatia." Although these people spoke Greek, they also spoke a Celtic dialect and were considered barbarians by some due to their history of warfare, their physical stature, and their strange language.

After years of conquest of and migration to this area by several different nations, the Romans took Galatia in 189 B.C. and created a large Roman province in 25 B.C. "Provincial Galatia" lay to the south of Old Galatia and was a much larger area, including the cities of Antioch, Iconium, Lystra, and Derbe and also parts of the regions of Phrygia, Pisidia, and Lycaonia. Although Tarsus, Paul's hometown, was in another region, it lay only about fifty miles southeast of Derbe.

We know from Acts that Paul visited Galatia. In Acts 13–14, we read of Paul's first missionary journey, which took him to the provincial Galatian city of Iconium and the region of Pisidia. Acts 16:1-8 gives us information about Paul's second missionary journey, from which I excerpt an itinerary: "Paul went on also to Derbe and to Lystra, where there was a disciple named Timothy. . . . He was well spoken of by the believers in Lystra and Iconium. . . . They [Paul and Timothy] went through the region of Phrygia and Galatia, having been forbidden by the Holy Spirit to speak the word in Asia. When they had come opposite Mysia, they attempted to go into Bithynia, but the Spirit of Jesus did not allow them; so, passing by Mysia, they went down to Troas." If you follow this route on a biblical map, you see that Paul and Timothy moved in a long curve from south central Asia Minor to the north-western city of Troas and onward to Macedonia in Greece. Later, after Paul left Greece, he visited Jerusalem and again visited Galatia. As Acts 18:23 puts it, "After spending some time there [in Antioch] he departed and went from place to place through the region of Galatia and Phrygia, strengthening all the disciples."

The Book of Acts never specifically says that Paul founded churches in Galatia, only that he "strengthened all the disciples" there. Some scholars believe that Paul founded churches in the western part of Old Galatia on his way to Bithynia during the second missionary journey. "After spending some time there" (perhaps a few years), as mentioned in Acts 18:23, Paul visited these churches again. (Galatians 4:13 implies more than one visit to the churches, according to some interpretations.) After he left, however, he heard of their troubles and wrote his letter. Although Acts 16:6 does not mention that Paul founded churches in Galatia, that can be explained by the haste of Paul and his companions in traveling through the region at the beckoning of the Holy Spirit. Thus we have the "North Galatia hypothesis," which maintains that Paul's letter was sent to churches in the Old Galatia region rather than in the southern Roman province.

Other scholars argue that Paul's churches were in South Galatia. These scholars say that Paul did, indeed, only pass through Phrygia and Galatia, as Acts 16:6 maintains, and that the silence of Acts concerning his activities means that Paul did not tarry long as the Spirit guided him to Troas and beyond. Paul was, after all, seriously ill when he first visited Galatia (Galatians 4:13-14). In addition, Paul typically used the names of Roman provinces when he referred to particular places in his letters. So when Paul wrote "to the churches in Galatia," he would have been thinking of the Roman province, not the region to the north.

The fact is, we do not know the location of the Galatian churches; both hypotheses have gained strong supporters. One must interpret the silence of Acts. Is the fact that Acts omits the founding of the Galatian churches significant? Where among Paul's itineraries reported in Acts does the Letter to the Galatians fit? Silence is notoriously difficult to interpret.

PAUL'S VISIT TO GALATIA

• Using a Bible atlas or the maps in your study Bible, locate the regions of Old Galatia and the greater Galatian region. Read Acts 13–14 and track the course of Paul's missionary journey on the Bible map. Then read Acts 15–18 and track that journey as well. Try to determine how far Paul traveled from one place to the next.

• What kinds of experiences did Paul have as he preached the good news of Christ? Are there any particular experiences that stand out for you? If so, which ones?

• Whether Paul established churches or just "strengthened the disciples," he clearly had a relationship with the congregations. Read Galatians 1:1-5 again and identify every element that Paul discloses about who he is. Then examine the verses for everything they say about Paul's theology. What do these few verses tell you about Paul and his relationship there?

• In your own spiritual growth, what have been your own "missionary journeys"? Have you had experiences or particular churches that were very meaningful to you? Have you had experiences (hearing a sermon or reading a book perhaps) that especially clarified to you the Christian gospel?

The Jerusalem Conference

Still another historical question is, Why didn't Paul mention the Jerusalem Conference in this letter? Reread Acts 15. The conference dealt with the very same matter as Paul's letter to the Galatians: "Certain individuals came down from Judea and were teaching the brothers, 'Unless you are circumcised according to the custom of Moses, you cannot be saved' " (Acts 15:1). According to Acts, Paul and Barnabas "had no small dissension and debate"

(Acts 15:2) with these individuals; and subsequently a conference was called at Jerusalem among the apostles and elders. The conference decided that "we should not trouble those Gentiles who are turning to God, but we should write to them to abstain only from things polluted by idols and from fornication and from whatever has been strangled and from blood" (Acts 15:19-20). These few dietary (kosher) and moral prescriptions—with circumcision noticeably absent—represented a minimum of older Jewish laws for Gentiles to observe. They reflected Jewish concern for humane treatment of animals (only animals killed painlessly are suitable to eat), for idolatry (we are called to worship the one God), and human relationships (our sexuality finds completion in the marriage commitment). The apostles sent a letter of recommendation with Paul and Barnabas, who had already evangelized the Gentiles, in case this matter of circumcision ever arose again (Acts 15:22-29).

One might think that, in Galatians, Paul would have called attention to the Jerusalem Conference in order to press his point that circumcision is of no value to Gentile Christians (Galatians 6:15). Yet he also failed to mention the conference in First Corinthians (written earlier), which deals with the matter of food offered to idols.

THE JERUSALEM CONFERENCE

• Read Acts 15. What was the purpose of this conference? What issues were at stake and who would be affected by the decision? What were the results?

• Why do you think the Jerusalem Conference selected these recommendations to the Gentile Christians? What do they signify? Why, do you think, did they not simply recommend the Ten Commandments?

• This conference is our first report of an organized effort to confront a "church fight." Who initiated the conference? How was it handled procedurally? What does this example teach us about dealing with misunderstanding or conflict in the church?
• Does your church have any stated or implicit "minimum requirements" for membership? What are they? What processes or procedures, if any, are there for accountability?

The Date of the Letter

When did Paul write the letter? Paul never dated any of his letters, so we have to guess when he wrote them based on hints from Acts and from the letters themselves. In Galatians, Paul never indicates his location.

So we return to the mystery of who were the Galatians. If one prefers the "South Galatia hypothesis," Galatians can be an early letter—as early as A.D. 49, around the time of Paul's Antioch journey in Acts 14:26. That may be one reason why he never mentions the Jerusalem Conference. Scholars date the conference between A.D. 49–51, and the Conference might have happened later than the letter. But if one assumes that Acts 18:23 refers to a journey to North Galatia, then the letter was probably written during the period 52 to 55—and Paul's silence about the Conference has other reasons known only to Paul. In Galatians he is careful to pay respect to the church leaders at Jerusalem while asserting his own God-given independence as a preacher.

Paul's letters appear in the New Testament according to their length: from the longest, Romans, to the tiny letter addressed to Philemon. But they were probably written in a very different order. Some scholars believe that Galatians is Paul's third letter—after First Thessalonians and First Corinthians but certainly before Romans, which is a more mature and complete statement of some of the same themes.

THE DATE OF THE LETTER

• All of Paul's correspondence is dated before any of the Gospels, so he obviously did not draw on their written content. (In fact, Paul was dead before Mark wrote the earliest Gospel in about A.D. 70.) Does the fact that Paul's correspondence and missionary activity reported in Acts pre-dates the written Gospels make you think any differently about how you use the Bible to understand the tenets and growth of Christianity? If so, how?

IN CLOSING

• Think about all the signs of covenant the people of faith have been given over the centuries. What signs of God's covenant with you are the most obvious and powerful?
• Offer prayer for all those who are, or who feel they are, outside of God's covenant of grace.

---

[1] From *Galatians*, by Charles B. Cousar, in **Interpretation** (Fortress Press, 1982); page 1.

[2] From *The Letters of Paul*, by Calvin J. Roetzel (Westminster John Knox Press, 1998); pages 53–54, 102.

[3] From *The Letters of Paul*; pages 52–54.

II A "SECOND STRING" APOSTLE?

No Other Gospel!
Read Galatians 1:6-10

Paul usually began his letters with a thanksgiving for the church to which he was writing, but he did not in the Letter to the Galatians. Read some first chapters among Paul's letters. For instance, in First Thessalonians he wrote, "We always give thanks to God for all of you and mention you in our prayers" (1 Thessalonians 1:2). "I give thanks to my God always for you because of the grace of God that has been given you in Christ Jesus" (1 Corinthians 1:4), he wrote to Corinth, a church with which he had several specific issues. "I thank my God through Jesus Christ for all of you, because your faith is proclaimed throughout the world" (Romans 1:8), wrote Paul to Rome, a church he had not visited.

Compare these warm words with the Letter to the Galatians. Paul skipped the thanksgiving entirely in Galatians and scolded them: "I am astonished that you are so quickly deserting the one who called you in the grace of Christ and are turning to a different gospel" (Galatians 1:6). One New Testament scholar, Nils Dahl, suggests that Paul, modifying the letter-writing conventions of his day for his own teaching purposes, replaced the thanksgiving with a rebuke. The Galatians would have been expecting a thanksgiving; they got something else.

One can imagine the congregation, who may have first known this text via a public reading, wondering, "What did we do that was so wrong? Isn't circumcision a *sine qua non*, that is, an indispensable rite, designating God's covenant with his people?" A few may have been put off by Paul's faintly condescending "astonishment." In this rebuke Paul quickly added, "not that there is another gospel" (Galatians 1:7). In other words, what the Galatians heard from Paul was the only gospel; and what they now had was no gospel at all. It was a confusion or a perversion of the true gospel (Galatians 1:8). His outrage was unrestrained. If Paul himself, or even an angel, should preach a different gospel than the gospel Paul had given them, "let that one be accursed" (Galatians 1:8-9). (The Greek word he used has passed into English as the word *anathema*.) As in Romans 9:1-5, Paul considered even his own salvation as dispensable if the gospel could be preached and could bring people to Christ.

NO OTHER GOSPEL!

• **If you did not already do so in the last chapter,** compare the introduction to Galatians to others in Paul's letters. What do these introductions tell us about Paul's purpose and his relationship with the congregations?

• What does Paul mean about "no other gospel"? Have you ever felt so strongly about your faith (or anything else) that you would sacrifice even yourself for the sake of another? If so, what was that experience like?

The Judaizers

To what was Paul reacting? "Judaizing" teachers had visited the churches at Galatia or perhaps resided with those congregations. We do not know exactly who these teachers at Galatia were. Consider this summary of Bible scholar Charles Cousar's contemporary research concerning the various possible identities of Paul's opponents at Galatia:

• Paul's opponents were Jewish Christians who said they had James' support and who represented the "circumcision party" at Jerusalem. These Jewish Christians believed Paul's teachings about freedom threatened the older Jewish ceremonial laws, which they maintained still applied to Christians.
• The Galatian teachers were not specifically connected with Jerusalem and basically supported Paul's teachings, except that his message needed the supplementation of circumcision.
• The teachers were syncretistic; that is, they were not specifically a Jerusalem-based group but, like Greek religion of the time, adopted aspects of other religions within their message. In this case, Jewish practices like festivals and circumcision mingled with their Christian teaching.
• The teachers were Gentile Christians who wanted to reintroduce circumcision to Paul's message, a practice they believed Paul had once upheld and then dropped.
• The teachers at Galatia were actually two groups with two different agendas: the practice of circumcision on the one hand and the transcendence of moral guides on the other. In other words, the second group of teachers were "antinomians," urging freedom from moral constraints.[1]

Whoever these teachers were, they maintained that a Christian must keep certain aspects of the old Mosaic law.

This was, as we saw earlier, a concern of many first-generation Christians. How much of the older Jewish law should Christians still uphold? What about Christian converts who were not previously Jewish? Jesus himself said, after all, "Do not think that I have come to abolish the law or the prophets; I have come not to abolish but to fulfill. For truly I tell you, until heaven and earth pass away, not one letter, not one stroke of a letter, will pass from the law until all is accomplished. Therefore, whoever breaks one of the least of these commandments, and teaches others to do the same, will be called least in the kingdom of heaven; but whoever does them and teaches them will be called great in the kingdom of heaven" (Matthew 5:17-19). (One must remember that Paul never appeals to Jesus' sayings when he teaches about the law.)

THE JUDAIZERS

• Using a Bible dictionary or commentary on Galatians 1:6-10, look up "Judaizers."
• Work through this list of possible identities. What would be the effect on the Galatian congregations and on Paul's work with them if the particular identity were true?
• There will always be persons in the church whose understandings and theology differ from yours. How does your congregation acknowledge differences and work with them?

Following the Law

"The law" and "the commandments" refer to the Torah, the first five books of the Bible. These books contain many stories and also many laws and commandments (traditionally numbered at 613, mostly found in Exodus through Deuteronomy). These laws and commandments were, and are, considered God-given and sacred material for Jews. (Read, for instance, Deuteronomy 4:1-2, 5-8; 6:1-9.) These Scriptures, among others, show how seriously the people were to take their obligation to observe God's laws.

Obedience to God's laws was one key aspect of Israel's covenant with God. This obedience is no rote, self-righteous legalism; this is the will of God revealed to God's people. God's laws are a great blessing and privilege (see, for instance, Psalm 119). As Israel observed the law, the Lord blessed, intervened on behalf of, and kept Israel because they were the least of all peoples (Deuteronomy 7:7-14).

The applicability of all the laws of the Torah has been an issue even within Judaism. Many of the laws are not applicable any longer. Today, Reform Jews, in the tradition of the Hebrew prophets, retain the Torah's moral laws while regarding the ceremonial laws as secondary or archaic. Reform Jews (reading, for instance, Amos 5:21-24, among other Scriptures) see the main purpose of the laws as creating justice and righteousness, not rote ceremony. Today, much more conservative Jews take Deuteronomy 4:2 and 13:1-4 literally and believe that, although Torah laws must be interpreted for each age, they should not be discarded. Like Christian groups, religious Jews find sincere differences among themselves concerning the interpretation of the ancient Scriptures.

As we will see shortly, Paul found his theological world thrown into confusion by his conversion. In Christ, he believed, we have a brand new thing that God has done. Now, he believed, Christians live by the Spirit and not by the Law. Through the Spirit we have the "righteousness [that] exceeds that of the scribes and the Pharisees" (Matthew 5:20), as Jesus put it. True, we do not discard the Law; and for the Jew, circumcision and the oracles of God are of great value (Romans 3:1-2). But at Galatia, most Christians were Gentiles. Given their background as "barbarians" in a Roman world, they would have welcomed the freedom and equality given them in Christ (Galatians 3:28). They had experienced the Spirit, and they were becoming "new creations." It was not necessary for them to become Jews, too, thus perpetuating the difference between Jews and non-Jews.

The teachers who had come to their congregations disagreed, however. No, God has commanded the people to be circumcised. Therefore you Galatian men need circumcision, too, they said, as a Jewish response to God's promises within your new lives as Christians. This was the situation to which Paul reacted so strongly. God had given them (and us) freedom and equal standing as children and heirs (Galatians 4:7), but they had misunderstood.

FOLLOWING THE LAW

• Read Deuteronomy 4:1-2, 5-8; 6:1-9; 7:7-14 to learn more about the Law and its importance. This is a major theme in Galatians. How would Paul's "theological world [be] thrown into confusion by his conversion"?
• What would be the importance of the Law (or lack of importance) to these "barbarian" Galatians?

Introducing Paul
Read Galatians 1:11–2:10

In this section Paul begins a long recapitulation of his background. He begins in verse 11 and continues through 2:14 (although for the rest of Chapter 2, he elaborates on his conflict with Peter). Why did Paul do this? He wanted to impress upon the Galatians that the gospel they received from him was from God. "I did not receive it from a human source, nor was I taught it, but I received it through a revelation of Jesus Christ" (Galatians 1:12). If the Galatians had any question about the gospel, they could be assured of Paul's authority. He was independent of the apostles in Jerusalem, although they also approved him.

When Paul says that "his" gospel was not of human origin, he does not mean he did not count on the help of others. Calvin Roetzel writes, "Elsewhere . . . Paul draws on church tradition, cites the primitive Christian kerygma [preaching], repeats liturgical formulas, quotes Christian hymns, prayers, and confessions, and uses traditional ethical admonitions." [2] Paul did not discount these human compositions from which he borrowed. Similarly, he was deeply indebted to Jewish traditions and to the Hellenistic world. But Paul states in no uncertain terms—for the benefit of the Galatians and the problem they were having and did not recognize—that his authority and message came from Christ. Paul's apostleship was of divine origin. "Am I now seeking human approval, or God's approval? . . . If I were still pleasing people, I would not be a servant of Christ" (Galatians 1:10).

Paul writes, interestingly, about his Christian experience. He does not describe for the Galatians his conversion on the road to Damascus, although he certainly could have. It is an impressive testimony, after all. Recall that Paul had traveled toward Damascus in order to expedite his persecution of Christians when a bright light knocked him to the ground. Christ revealed himself to Paul; and following three days of fasting and blindness, Paul was baptized and began preaching Jesus in the Damascus synagogues (Acts 9:1-22). In Galatians, Paul merely states that he received the gospel through a revelation of Christ.

INTRODUCING PAUL

• Read Galatians 1:11-2:10. What does Paul tell about himself? If he had founded the congregation, might the members have known this about him already? Regardless, what does Paul want to clarify to them about himself and his relationship to God? to them?

Paul's Gospel of Jesus Christ

What is the gospel of Jesus? In his writings (to cite just a few examples), Paul calls attention to several aspects of the good news:

• God's justification and redemption of us (Romans 3:21-26)
• The satisfaction of God's justice by Christ's perfect sacrifice for our violations of God's law (Romans 3:23-26)
• Forgiveness of our sins through the blood of the cross (Romans 5:8-9)
• Reconciliation between God and us through Christ (Romans 5:10-11)
• A new covenant based on grace rather than on works of the law (Romans 5:20-21)
• The assurance of God's free gift of mercy and salvation at the Final Judgment (Romans 6:23; 8:1-2)
• God's promise never to forsake us and God's promise never to allow anything to separate us from God's love (Romans 8:31-39)
• God's promise to continue working in our lives to establish holiness and love (1 Corinthians 6:9-11)

- A mortal blow against the powers of evil in the world (1 Corinthians 15:24-28)
- The defeat of the power of sin and death through Christ's resurrection (1 Corinthians 15:51-57)
- The eventual transformation of our mortal, physical bodies into spiritual, eternal bodies (1 Corinthians 15:51-57)
- The removal of barriers that separate us (Galatians 3:27-29; Ephesians 2:14-16)
- The assurance that we are God's beloved children in Christ (Galatians 4:7)
- God's identification with human suffering and death through the self-emptying of Jesus (Philippians 2:5-8)

For this kind of good news, Paul redirected everything in his life in order to proclaim Jesus Christ to everyone who would listen to him.

PAUL'S GOSPEL OF JESUS CHRIST

- In three or four teams, divide this list. Look up the Scriptures. Then together, discuss the total scope of Paul's gospel. Which of these teachings is (or are) the most transformational and personally empowering? Why? How do these aspects of the good news shape your life?
- Note the particular themes in this list that are emphasized in Galatians. How are these themes important in your faith? How might they have influenced a congregation of "barbarians"? of persons with quite a different history? of persons caught between old habits and beliefs and new teachings that are opposite or incompatible?
- Imagine that you are part of a newly created mission team to head to [country of your choice]. What are the theological truths that you would find most important to try to convey? In an attitude of respect to the receiving culture, how would you begin to establish your relationship with the host country?

Paul, the Pharisee

"You have heard, no doubt, of my earlier life in Judaism," Paul writes in Galatians 1:13. We recall his self-description in Philippians 3:5-6: "circumcised on the eighth day, a member of the people of Israel, of the tribe of Benjamin, a Hebrew born of Hebrews; as to the law, a Pharisee; as to zeal, a persecutor of the church; as to righteousness under the law, blameless." According to Acts 22:3 (although the fact is never mentioned by Paul himself in his letters), he studied Torah in Jerusalem under the illustrious rabbi Gamaliel. If Paul felt conflict within his own soul as to the difficulty of keeping righteousness by the law (Romans 7:7-25), he nevertheless excelled in religious observance and took great pride in his background. He was a member of the tribe of Benjamin and named for King Saul. His name in Latin, *Paulus*, would have been his name as a Roman citizen.

We know much about the Pharisees from the Gospels, Calvin Roetzel writes:

> Although the picture of the Pharisees painted by the Gospel writers is a distortion of historical reality [based on church-synagogue tensions of the time], much that is historically reliable can be learned about the Pharisees from the Gospels. From them we learn about the Pharisaic emphasis on ritualistic purity. Careful to eat the right kind of foods, to purify (not merely wash) vessels used in food preparation, and to exclude the unclean (such as tax collectors and prostitutes) from table fellowship, the Pharisees obviously treated all of life as a ritual. Unlike the priests who took the laws of Leviticus relating to sacrifice, eating temple food, and cultic preparation to apply only to the temple itself and its worship, for the Pharisees the "setting for law observance was the field and the kitchen, the bed and the street." Taking quite literally the command in Exodus 19:6 to be a "kingdom of priests," the Pharisees attempted to act as if all of the common life was a temple service.[3]

Although Paul counted his earlier religious observance as "loss" (Philippians 3:7), he by no means abandoned his background. In many ways he only modified it in light of the great fact of Christ. Paul spoke positively about his own Pharisaism in Acts 25:8 and Acts 26:4-5. He shared many Pharisaic ideas: the resurrection of the righteous, the rabbinical method of interpreting Scripture, his refusal to stand aloof from everyday matters, his combined beliefs in God's providence and also human ethical responsibility. But he also associated with Gentiles, abandoned "laws of purity," and adopted a very different belief in the Messiah than traditional Jews. "Certainly by the strictest interpretation," writes Roetzel, "Paul appears to compromise his Pharisaic tradition, but to say that he rejected it outright is going too far. It would be more accurate to say that Paul's letters reflect a fresh appraisal of those traditions in light of his conviction that in the cross and resurrection of Jesus God's final eschatological breakthrough was occurring."[4] Paul took aim at the strictness of the Pharisees because their devotion had the effect of erecting barriers between them (the ones who could keep the law) and others (those who could not, either because they were sinners or were Gentiles).

PAUL, THE PHARISEE

• Using a Bible dictionary, look up "Pharisee." How does this information augment what is in this text?

• Read the several Scriptures in which Paul mentions his credentials. How would his lifelong religious practices bump up against his associations with Gentiles?

• We often think of the Pharisees as rigid, rule-bound, and unnecessarily favoring the letter over the spirit of the Law. Yet, Paul had to be flexible in dealing with an almost exclusive Gentile audience. How have your personal codes, beliefs, and practices been challenged in the name of faith? How often do you encounter a situation that challenges, stretches, or even threatens what you believe? How much are you willing to bend?

How do you establish the faith and practice boundaries that you will not cross?

Early Travels

Paul states that he went to Arabia following his conversion and then returned to Damascus. The Book of Acts implies that he visited Jerusalem fairly soon after his conversion, which occurred around A.D. 35 when he was about 25; but his own account states otherwise. Only after his sojourns in Arabia (the area of Petra) and Damascus, did he go to Jerusalem in about A.D. 37, where he visited Peter for fifteen days. Paul is emphatic about this point: He visited only Peter (whose name in the Aramaic language is *Cephas*) and James when he went to Jerusalem. "In what I am writing to you, before God, I do not lie!" (Galatians 1:20). Paul wanted to impress upon the Galatians his independence from the apostles.

Why did Paul go to these places? Perhaps he went to Arabia in order to be alone with God in light of this momentous change in his life. As far as Damascus is concerned, that was the place to which he journeyed when Christ touched his life so dramatically. In finally arriving in Damascus, Paul completed a delayed journey in very different circumstances. It was a courageous journey. Who would believe him there? Paul, the man who once persecuted Christians, was now one himself.

Following that visit, he went to Syria and Cilicia for fourteen years. That journey, too, would have been difficult; Tarsus, his hometown, was located in Cilicia. Jesus said, "Prophets are not without honor except in their own country and in their own house" (Matthew 13:57). What experiences did Paul have among his own people? Were they proud of him? skeptical? hostile? Paul states that he did not visit the churches of Judea at all; but they "glorified God" (Galatians 1:24) because of him, not because he met them, but because they heard about him.

After fourteen years in his own land, Paul went again to Jerusalem, around A.D. 49–51, along with Barnabas and Titus. Once again, Paul had the courage to return to an area where he was known as a persecutor of Christians and as a traitor to Judaism. In this passage, however, he is not boasting of his courage but of proving his qualified independence from the Jerusalem church. I say "qualified" because Paul wanted to show the Galatians that he was by no means against the leaders at Jerusalem. In fact, he wanted to show his respect. He wanted to receive their respect and approbation while, at the same time, he refused to bend his own God-given message to potential pressure. "I went up [to Jerusalem] in response to a revelation. Then I laid before them (though only in a private meeting with the acknowledged leaders) the gospel that I proclaim among the Gentiles, in order to make sure I was not running, or had not run, in vain" (Galatians 2:2). This seems to be the meeting mentioned in Acts 15:2.

EARLY TRAVELS

• Using a Bible atlas or a map in your study Bible, trace these travels of Paul and note his approximate age at the time of his experiences and visits. (He was born about A.D. 10.)

• Sketch out some "highlights" of your own spiritual journey, including significant locations. How may our own spiritual and geographical journeys reflect a Christian experience similar (or dissimilar) to Paul's?

• If Peter, James, and John were Jesus' age, give or take a few years (and we don't know that), they could have been at least fifteen years older than Paul. We know our life expectancy and life rhythm are different from the biblical era; nevertheless, think about what you were doing at the same age as when Paul had his various experiences and encounters. Did you have a dramatic conversion experience? If so, at what age? At what age or level of maturity and experience did you assume a leadership role in your church? How would you feel, or have felt, confronting a "Council at Jerusalem experience" at age forty? How would you feel, or have felt, taking on a noted church leader like Peter, who was your elder?

Paul's Authority

The leaders at Jerusalem included Peter, James, and John, "who were [the] acknowledged pillars" of the church and who "recognized the grace that had been given to me [Paul]" (Galatians 2:9). The translation "those who were supposed to be acknowledged leaders" (Galatians 2:6) echoes older translations ("reputed to be pillars"), which also sounds mildly sarcastic. Perhaps Paul is making a point here. Peter, James, and John were popular leaders; but who empowers Christian leadership? God, who "shows no partiality" (Galatians 2:6), is the source of the gospel, regardless of who occupies positions of leadership. James was respected in Jerusalem by both disputing "camps": the Christians, who did not believe in the need for circumcision, and the "Judaizers," who opposed too much Gentile influence in the Christian faith.

Paul stressed the fact that the Jerusalem leaders extended fellowship to him and agreed that he, Paul, should preach to the Gentiles as he had been doing. Their only request was "that we remember the poor, which was actually what I was eager to do" (Galatians 2: 10). "The poor" were Christians in Jerusalem (or elsewhere in that area of Judea) for whom Paul took a collection, as mentioned in Acts 11:29-30; Romans 15:26; 1 Corinthians 16:1-3; 2 Corinthians 8:1-5.

The issue was important for the Galatians to understand. God certainly showed "no partiality" in selecting Paul as an apostle. In fact, many people would have (and did) considered Paul at the very least a "second string" apostle, at worst a self-aggrandizing phony. The "apostles" were those who were with Jesus during his earthly ministry. Paul did not qualify. When Judas died, the remaining apostles sought divine guidance and selected Matthias, a witness to the Resurrection, as the group's last new addition (Acts 1:21-26).

Paul became an apostle through the direct intervention of God. Paul was conscious of the fact that he, a persecutor of the church, was surely not the most likely choice. But God's will was done! God chose Paul as an apostle! The church at Jerusalem understood this, and so they gave Paul their respect and approval as he ministered to the Gentiles. Paul told this to the Galatians so they might understand his authority to preach to them the true gospel—unlike the teachers who recently visited the church.

Because of Paul's God-given authority, "false believers" were "secretly brought in" and "slipped in to spy on the freedom we have in Christ Jesus" (Galatians 2:4). Sneaky people can still be found in churches. Too insecure and weak to deal with matters in the light, they watch what others do and then gossip and find fault. They hope to run things, but seldom in a forthright, true manner. Paul proudly noted that "we did not submit to them even for a moment, so that the truth of the gospel might always remain with you" (Galatians 2:5).

PAUL'S AUTHORITY

• Review Galatians 2:1-10 again. How does this passage reflect the church leadership and their credentials? Paul's credentials?
• How, do you think, might the acknowledged leaders have received Paul, knowing that in his youth, he had dedicated his life to persecuting Christians? knowing that he had been converted and now zealously supported what he had once vigorously condemned?
• How do you deal with transformations in the lives of others important to you? Are you able to let go of old impressions and make new ones? to trust those who once were untrustworthy but now seem to have established their fidelity? to support younger, but qualified, leaders?

IN CLOSING

• Offer prayer for those who give their lives to the very often dangerous mission field and for the wisdom and insight necessary to seize personal opportunities to share the faith.

[1] From *Galatians*, by Charles B. Cousar, in **Interpretation** (John Knox, 1982); pages 5–6

[2] From *The Letters of Paul*, by Calvin J. Roetzel (Westminster John Knox Press, 1998); page 67.

[3] From *The Letters of Paul*; pages 37-38.

[4] From *The Letters of Paul*; pages 39-40.

III FAITH OR WORKS?

A Difficult Personality
Read Galatians 2:11-14

Paul fascinates us. Sometimes he was confrontational and fearless, sometimes he worried that he appeared humble and weak to people and that he finally became bold in his letters (2 Corinthians 10:1, 10). He referred to his background as "loss," also translated as "rubbish" though literally the term refers to human waste (Philippians 3:8), but was also proud of it (Philippians 3:4-6). He disliked the idea of female leadership in churches—or at least of women speaking in church (1 Corinthians 14:34-35)—while praising the work of particular women among the churches (Romans 16:1, 3, 6, 12-15; Philippians 4:2-3). He recommends to the churches, "Be imitators of me" (1 Corinthians 11:1)—meaning, "Have the kind of Christlike humility and love that I strive for"—but his words give the wrong impression of egotism even as he points to humility as the virtue one should emulate.

Paul had a difficult time with opponents and even with friends. Some of this surely had to do with the greatness of his purpose, his devotion to Christ, and his uncompromising fidelity to his Lord. Paul was an "enormous" apostle, and therefore he attracted the littler people who wanted to tear down rather than build up.

Paul's sense of mission, and apparently his personality, had a certain alienating quality. He was a former persecutor who sometimes criticized others very harshly. He expended many words vindicating his own ministry (as in the Galatians passages we just read and also in 2 Corinthians 1–7; 10–13). Sometimes it seems, as Shakespeare put it, he "doth protest too much," as Paul's comments appear to cross into excessive hurt and defensiveness. (In other words, Paul was very human.)

In the case of Second Corinthians, he defended himself against those whom he sarcastically called "super-apostles" (2 Corinthians 11:5), "deceitful workers, disguising themselves as apostles of Christ. And no wonder! Even Satan disguises himself as an angel of light" (2 Corinthians 11:13-14). We should not emulate Paul, of course, in so naming people with whom we disagree. Second Timothy ends on the very sad note that several of Paul's friends and associates have abandoned him (2 Timothy 4:9-17).

Calvin Roetzel comments, "[Paul's] adjurations are especially harsh to our modern ears. They sound mean and vindictive. Yet they are understandable in terms of Paul's sense of his mission. Paul felt himself to be like the prophets of old, who were commissioned to speak the word of Yahweh. . . . Paul, believing himself appointed as an apostle of the risen Christ, felt he re-presented Christ to his hearers for judgment and healing; and thus, in his view, the words he spoke had the power and authority of the one who sent him."[1]

Somehow Peter comes across to us as more lovable. He was not without his own harshness, however. Paul never cut off anyone's ear, for instance, although he wished his opponents at Galatia would castrate themselves (Galatians 5:12). So far as we know, Paul did not deny Christ when pressured, although his earlier persecution of Christians surely plagued his mind.

A DIFFICULT PERSONALITY

• What have been your impressions of Paul in your study experience? Have you noticed these seeming contradictions or wide range of acceptability on issues?
• Read the supporting Scriptures. How does Paul's portrait emerge for you now?
• Do you agree or disagree that Paul was an "enormous apostle" and that his ministry "had a certain alienating quality"? Why? Does it make any difference to you in terms of Paul's authenticity as a spokesman for the faith?
• Is the role today of clergy or missionaries to speak with the power and authority of the one who called and sent them? Explain. What does that mean to you? How do you understand that power and authority? Do you feel that you could ever speak with the weight of God's authority? In what circumstance or setting?

A Matter of Table Fellowship

Paul was not only a prophet in the sense of the uncompromising preacher. He was also a prophet in the way he sided with the less fortunate, affirming their closeness to God. Paul stood up for those who would be excluded from Christian fellowship. He showed wonderful love and understanding, as well as courage, in his relationships with his "parishioners." Sometimes Paul wore his heart on his sleeve, which also made him very human. The Letter to the Galatians is an example of this. Imagine someone who is close to you. Then imagine that person does not listen to your advice about some matter but does listen to someone much less close to him or her. That can be a hurtful, exasperating situation; and in this letter Paul reacts humanly to that very thing.

In Galatians 2:11-14, Paul continues his recollections from our earlier passage. He has told the Galatians that the pillars of the church (Peter, James, and John) recognized God's grace in his ministry and extended to him fellowship and respect. Although Paul was not an "original" apostle, he was a true apostle through God.

The matter did not end there, however. Paul later met Peter at Antioch. Peter had had table fellowship with both Jews and Gentiles; but at Antioch, Peter was criticized by "certain people . . . from James" (Galatians 2:12) for eating with Gentiles. Peter then withdrew from Gentile Christians "for fear of the circumcision faction" (Galatians 2:12) and did not eat with the Gentiles. Even Barnabas and other Jewish converts were swayed by the pressure and withdrew from the Gentiles.

In part this was a matter of Christian table fellowship, which Paul stressed was a matter of Christian love. Read 1 Corinthians 11:17-34. In the ancient Greek world, the evening meal was often a very social occasion. One ate the large meal with one's family and social contacts. There was no time schedule, so everyone sat and talked for a long time. The diners were happily present to one another without competing obligations. This custom translated easily into the early Christian fellowship known as a "love feast." Often the Lord's Supper was shared along with the social meal. The social meal itself demonstrated the universality of Christ's salvation. People of all social and economic classes met together, even though they might not meet in other social situations. The rich and poor alike shared in the Christian feast, just as they shared in Christ's salvation.

In First Corinthians, Paul upbraided that church for its factions and for its factional spirit. The members of the congregation too easily divided themselves into "in groups." They were a congregation easily impressed with certain types of big, bold leadership—the kind of leadership Paul did not claim to exercise—and with certain types of people. So the wealthier and socially higher people at Corinth began to dominate these love feasts, eating up the food and drinking all the wine. The poorer people went hungry and could not enjoy the dinner. Furthermore (as happens in many churches where certain people are the movers and shakers), the "higher ups" at Corinth were oblivious to their thoughtlessness toward those who deserved equal fellowship.

This kind of behavior, Paul wrote to the Corinthians, is not only impolite but is also antithetical to the gospel! (This is the meaning of his often misunderstood warning in 1 Corinthians 11:27 about taking the Lord's Supper "in an unworthy manner," not that one must be morally perfect to take Communion.) At table fellowship, one should be aware both of the presence of Christ and of his concern (that we must share) for those who have less.

A MATTER OF TABLE FELLOWSHIP

• Read Galatians 2:11-14. What are the issues at stake here?
• Read 1 Corinthians 11:17-34. What are the issues at stake?
• Imagine a dinner at your own church. What are the expectations about who is welcome and how the meal should be prepared, served, and received? Is there anyone who is not welcome? If so, why? What beliefs, behaviors, or decisions about the dinner could be divisive or start a conflict?
• How does Christian fellowship find its "apex" in fellowship over a meal? Who is welcomed at the Lord's Supper? Is anyone excluded? If so, why?
• What might be "an unworthy manner" in which to share Communion or any other fellowship meal? What makes it unworthy?

Conflict With Peter

This is one reason why Paul became incensed with Peter at Antioch. That is, by withdrawing from the Gentiles, Peter essentially denied that they were genuine Christians too. You can put yourself in Peter's place, feeling anxiety about the "circumcision faction" who associated themselves with Peter's friend James. Peter found himself between the proverbial Scylla and Charybdis, or between "a rock and a hard place." But we can more readily sympathize with the Gentile Christians who were conceivably hurt and confused by the sudden aloofness of Jewish Christians like Peter and Barnabas.

One may also praise Paul for the way in which he handled this situation. When he met the leaders at Jerusalem, he did so privately and respectfully. When he criticized Peter, he did so to his face. Paul did not sneak around and talk about Peter behind his back. He did not equivocate. Paul took the side of the Gentiles who were excluded from table fellowship rather than be silent and avoid criticism from the "higher ups." One assumes that in this passage Paul wanted to make an implicit point, for the situations at Antioch and Galatia were parallel.

In both cases a "circumcision party" had come in and pressed their issue in a clandestine manner that created barriers between people rather than building up the Christian community. In both cases the Gentile Christians were made to feel diminished, made to feel that they were "second class" Christians behind the Jewish Christians. In both cases Paul, a renowned Jewish scholar and leader, took the side of the Gentile community. The Galatians—who were considered to be "barbarians" by the surrounding Roman society— should have understood how the Antioch Gentiles felt.

However, the matter of the Jewish law came into play as well in this dispute. William Barclay paraphrases Paul's response in Galatians 2:14: "You shared table with the Gentiles; you ate as they ate; therefore you approved in principle that there is one way for Jew and Gentile alike. How can you now reverse your decision and want the Gentiles to be circumcised and take the law upon them?" [2]

Sometimes people are legalistic but fall into sin themselves. You may know people, or can think of people, who have been vocal in their criticisms and condemnations of others yet have fallen into some kind of sin themselves. Therefore we must always be careful in how we judge others, as Paul cautions the Galatians (6:1-5). When we begin to impose rules and restrictions on others, we sometimes find ourselves behaving inconsistently. When Peter began to fall back into old ways of thinking, he acted toward the Gentiles in a manner he would have opposed when his attitude was more open and loving.

One may speculate what happened to Peter and Paul's relationship after this incident. We do not know Peter's side of the story. He may have had a different "take" on the situation.

One may also speculate about what Peter thought of Paul. Peter, of course, shared many moments with Jesus: happy ones, difficult ones, times of distress and privation, times of friendship and danger. Peter was "the rock," the one whose faith is the basis of Christ's church (Matthew 16:17-18). Did Peter resent Paul as an apostle-after-the-fact? Did he feel camaraderie with a fellow Jew who also occasionally ended up in jail for his beliefs? Tradition holds that both men were executed in Rome around the mid-60s.

CONFLICT WITH PETER

• Imagine the confrontation of Paul with Peter. What do you think happened after Paul and Peter quarreled? Might Peter have been doing as Paul said he did by trying to be all things to all people? What difference would that make, if any?

• Paul essentially accused Peter of hypocrisy and of thereby leading astray one of his own protegees, Barnabas. When, if ever, is it appropriate to behave in one way in a particular situation and another way in some other circumstance?

• How did Paul handle the situation? Is that a good model to follow today? Explain.

• In pairs or threes, think of some "rock and a hard place" situations you have experienced in work, church, school, or with family. How do you decide what to do? What role does prayer or other forms of Christian guidance play in that decision making? How do you deal with the "fallout" that comes, no matter what you decide?

• In what situations does God call us (or you, personally) to speak with boldness? What price are you willing to pay for that boldness?

"No Longer I Who Live, But . . . Christ"
Read Galatians 2:15-21

In this section we find the great principle of Paul's letter — and of his gospel. Some commentators maintain that verses 15-16 complete the comment Paul made to Peter that began in verse 14. (The Greek text has no quotation marks.) Still other Bible scholars maintain that this section is merely an elaboration, not a quotation. Whichever is the case, Paul comes to a grand point in these sentences.

They are not always easy sentences to unravel, however. In the tradition of Paul's Pharisaism, he formerly believed that the law must permeate the whole of life. But this created a division between the "law-keepers" and those who would not or could not observe all the rules and regulations. Remember the people to whom Jesus ministered: tax collectors, prostitutes, Samaritans, people with illnesses, and common workers. One way or another, these people broke the law because of moral failings, or by having spiritually "unclean" diseases, or because their lives could not be spent on full-time adherence to the law. When Paul says, "We ourselves are Jews by birth and not Gentile sinners" (Galatians 2:15), he evokes a traditional Jewish attitude of the day to hark back to this distinction. Anyone who violated something the law commanded was a sinner. People like the Gentiles who did not have the law were also sinners, even though God blessed the nations of the world through the Hebrew people (Genesis 12:1-3).

Through Christ, however, we are justified through faith rather than through works of the law (Galatians 2:16). Although the law can conceivably be kept in its entirety (Paul himself is an example of one who could and did.), the law does not contain the power to enable one to share in God's Spirit. The law does not give us the power to overcome sin (Romans 7:14-25). The law cannot make us alive. Christ became a "sinner" under the provisions of the law in order that we might be saved by him and not by works of the law. (Paul elaborates these points later in the letter.)

"But if, in our effort to be justified in Christ, we ourselves have been found to be sinners, is Christ then a servant of sin? Certainly not!" (Galatians 2:17). One could interpret this verse in at least two ways: If we discover through Christ that we are sinners according to the law, then is Christ the cause of our sin? No! Rather, Christ shows to us that salvation through observance of the law is truly impossible; therefore we accept his love of us sinners and his free gift of salvation. We accept his healing of our sin and his help. But the fact that Christ shows us to be sinners does not mean Christ "causes" us to be sinners.

We can also interpret this verse in this way: Although salvation is not through works, we cannot use our freedom in Christ in order to fall back into sin. True, we can and do sin even though we are justified in Christ. But that does not mean Christ is the cause or reason for our sin. Christ heals us of our sin as we continue in our walk with him. This, too, Paul elaborates later in Galatians.

One of the most beautiful passages in the Bible, in my opinion, is found in Galatians 2:19-20: "I have been crucified with Christ; and it is no longer I who live, but it is Christ who lives in me. And the life I now live in the flesh I live by faith in the Son of God, who loved me and gave himself for me." The King James Version translates it slightly more poetically: "I live, yet not I, but Christ liveth in me."

Before, Paul had lived a life of obedience. But there is a fine line—one that both Jews and Christians walk—between obedience as a response to God's grace and obedience as a way to earn God's pleasure. For Paul, the inability of the law to make us alive and free is a drastic problem, one so serious that we need nothing less than God's Son to save us. But Christ's power is so much greater than the law, providing us with nothing less than the Spirit of the almighty God, that Paul would no longer claim anything of his own. He had died to the law but had come to life in Christ. The law is no "respirator" if we are already "dead" to sin. In both the Old and New Testaments, only God can give us breath and life.

NO LONGER I WHO LIVE

• Read Galatians 2:15-21. Recall and review how the Pharisees regarded and observed the law.
• What are the distinctions here between those who follow the law and those who don't?
• The law does not have the power to save, but it does serve a purpose. How would you describe that purpose? What else does and does not the law do?
• Now sort out the two ways we might interpret Galatians 2:17. First (Christ is not the cause of our sin), how does Christ show us that we are sinners according to the law? What does that mean? What is the nature, then, of Christ's salvation?
• Second (our freedom in Christ is no excuse to sin), if we cannot hope to keep the whole law, is there any point in trying to follow any of it? What, for Christians, is the law? If salvation is not through works, what purpose is there in doing good works? If grace and salvation are freely given, what point is there in trying to keep from sin?
• What does it mean that "Christ lives in you"? Do you feel that is so for you? What difference, if any, does it make in your daily life? in your work? in your family? in your participation in a faith community?

Living in Two Different Times

Paul sees Christians as living in two different times: the present and the future. The past is canceled, for "while we still were sinners Christ died for us" (Romans 5:8). The future is already ours; eternal life with and through Christ finds fulfillment in the future but is available for us right now. The tricky part is the present. "Do not let sin exercise dominion in your mortal bodies" (Romans 6:12), Paul advises, because Christ has already defeated sin so that we might not be enslaved to it (Romans 6:5-10). We do, however, continue to sin. "So you also must consider yourselves dead to sin and alive to God in Christ Jesus" (Romans 6:11) because, in fact, Christ's life is ours, now and forever.

It is worth recalling Romans 1–3 at this point. Paul probably wrote Romans sometime soon after Galatians, for the two letters share many themes. While Galatians is full of worried outrage at people Paul knew personally, Romans is a more reasoned argument written for a church Paul had never visited. Paul argues that the Gentiles should have known and acknowledged God but did not act on that knowledge (Romans 1:18-32). The Jew has the law but runs the risk of being judged by the law when he or she sins (Romans 2). Though circumcision and the law are advantageous, and "real circumcision is a matter of the heart" (2:29), Jews find themselves under the power of sin as do Gentiles (3:9-20). Thus we are justified through Jesus Christ alone (3:21-31). He condemned the sin under which Jews and Gentiles suffer (8:3) so that truly our sin is crucified in him (Galatians 2:19). Now we are justified, not by the law that would condemn us, but by the free grace of God in Christ (2:20-21).

LIVING IN TWO DIFFERENT TIMES

• Discuss Paul's sense of his own identity. What about him changed when he became a Christian? What stayed the same?

• Read Romans 1–3 and the selected other passages in Romans 5–6 to get a sense of how this letter reiterates and clarifies some of the themes in Galatians. "Sin" for Paul means failure of the creature (us) to acknowledge the power and sovereignty of the Creator (God) and the subsequent alienation of creature from Creator (Romans 1:18-32).

• How do we live both as sinners and as saved people? The list of trans-gressions in Roman 1:29-32 is evidence of sin (alienation from God). How do these transgressions separate us from God? How do we avail ourselves of Christ's power so that sin does not reign in us?

• In what ways are Christians "crucified with Christ"? Do we ever leave our old life wholly behind us? How do we allow his divine life to live in us today?

Luther and Wesley

Two great Christian thinkers took different approaches to this text (Galatians 2:19-20). Listen to Martin Luther in his commentary on Galatians:

> "I do not speak," he says in effect, "about my death and crucifixion as though I do not now live. I do live, for I have been brought to life by Christ's death and crucifixion, through which I die. That is, forasmuch as I have been set free from the law, sin, and death, I am now truly alive. Therefore my crucifixion and death to the law, sin, death, and all evils is resurrection and life to me, for Christ crucifies the devil. He kills death, condemns sin, and binds the law; and I believe this and am set free from the law, sin, death, and the devil. . . ."
>
> The apostle shows what Christian righteousness is—namely, the righteousness by which Christ lives in us, and not the righteousness that is in our person. 3

If we start looking at our own righteousness, says Luther, who we are and how imperfect we are and how much growth we need, then we lose sight of Christ whose righteousness is ours.

John Wesley, the father of Methodism, takes a different approach. In his brief book *A Plain Account of Christian Perfection*, he writes,

> Every one of these [Christians] can say, with St. Paul, 'I am crucified with Christ; nevertheless I live; yet not I, but Christ liveth in me;'—words that manifestly describe a deliverance from inward as well as from outward sin. This is expressed both negatively, 'I live not,' my evil nature, the body of sin, is destroyed; and positively, 'Christ liveth in me,' and therefore all that is holy, and just, and good. Indeed, both these, 'Christ liveth in me,' and, 'I live not,' are inseparably connected. For what communion hath light with darkness, or Christ with Belial?
>
> He, therefore, who liveth in these Christians hath 'purified their hearts by faith;' insomuch that every one that has Christ in him,

'the hope of glory, purifieth himself even as he is pure.' He is puri-
fied from pride; for Christ was lowly in heart: He is pure from
desire and self-will; for Christ desired only to do the will of his
Father: And he is pure from anger, in the common sense of the
word; for Christ was meek and gentle. I say, in the common sense
of the word; for he is angry at sin, while he is grieved for the sinner. He feels a displacency at every offence against God, but only
tender compassion to the offender.

Thus doth Jesus save his people from their sins, not only from
outward sins, but from the sins of their hearts. . . .

Exactly agreeable to this are [John's] words in the first chapter
[of 1 John]: 'God is light, and in him is no darkness at all. If we
walk in the light, as he is in the light, we have fellowship one with
another, and the blood of Jesus Christ his Son cleanseth us from
all sin.' And again: 'If we confess our sins, he is faithful and just to
forgive us our sins, and to cleanse us from all unrighteousness.' [4]

For Luther, we never really have a righteousness of our
own. "It is no longer I who live, but it is Christ who lives
in me" (Galatians 2:20). All that matters is Christ's life,
which fills us, guides us, and saves us. Our obedience is
really as nothing compared to the greatness of Christ within
us. But for Wesley, Christ takes a more active role in
"improving" us. Christ cleanses us of our unrighteousness
as we strive to walk with him and to be faithful to his life.
Yet for Wesley, this is not being "saved by works." This is
wholly a life of the Spirit. Although we do seek to be obedient to him, it is God's initiative that makes us holy and
gives us fellowship with other people.

Thus Paul's beautiful statement, "The life I now live in
the flesh I live by faith in the Son of God, who loved me
and gave himself for me" (Galatians 2:20).

LUTHER AND WESLEY

• Discuss (or roleplay) the different positions of Luther and Wesley. One says, "I have no righteousness except Christ's; therefore I am always in some sense a sinner." The other says, "Christ's righteousness cleanses me of my sin so that, although I am never ever perfect, I can have a holiness of my own, initiated by Christ."

• How do you understand holiness and righteousness? What does it mean to you to be saved from sin?

• How do you understand yourself as a participant in the crucifixion and resurrection of Jesus the Christ? What difference does that make in your understanding of your faith and how to live out that faith?

IN CLOSING

• Take some time to reflect on the meaning of the law and of Christ living in you. How can and does your faith in Jesus Christ shape, even transform, your life?

• Offer prayers for all persons who are oppressed by unnecessary or unjust laws or regulations.

---

[1] From *The Letters of Paul*, by Calvin J. Roetzel (Westminster John Knox Press, 1998); pages 63–64.

[2] From *The Letters to the Galatians and Ephesians*, by William Barclay (Westminster Press, 1976); page 20.

[3] From *Galatians*, by Martin Luther (Crossway Books, 1998); page 105.

[4] From "A Plain Account of Christian Perfection," by John Wesley, in *The Works of John Wesley*, Volume 11, edited by Thomas Jackson (Wesleyan Methodist Book Room); page 377.

IV FAITH CAME FIRST

Receiving the Spirit
Read Galatians 3:1-5

What does Abraham mean to you? He is revered by three world religions (Judaism, Christianity, and Islam), representing nearly two billion people, as the father of faith in the one God. In Galatians 3, Paul continues his main point: God saves by faith rather than by works. Paul uses different arguments to prove his point. First he uses the example of experience. Then he uses the example of Abraham.

Read Acts 3:1-10; 8:14-17; 10:44-48. In these passages we read that early Christians received gifts of the Spirit when they came to faith. This was evidence of the Spirit's power. Even at the Jerusalem Conference, the evidence of the Spirit among the Gentiles conformed to scriptural promise (Acts 15:13-18). What God had done through the Spirit was seen and known, then understood to be consistent with Scripture.

Remember that, during the time of the early church, no "New Testament" existed. Christians (both Jew and Gentile) had to figure out what God was doing. My former professor, the New Testament scholar Luke Timothy Johnson, likes to say that theology is a game of "catch up." We try to catch up with the great things that God is doing. In the early church, evidences of the Spirit had to be observed and understood in the proper way. Leaders like Paul helped Christians understand the mighty works of God which, possibly, were not readily understandable.

When Paul introduced the gospel to the Galatians, they apparently received the Spirit in some tangible or observable way (Galatians 3:4-5). That gift of the Spirit proved (or should have proved) that God's salvation comes apart from works of the law. The Galatians were Gentiles, but they now had been included among God's own people! This would have been (or should have been) a momentous, liberating experience. The noted commentator Hans Dieter Betz writes, "Being 'barbarians' they may not have had great difficulty in rejecting the distinction between Greek and Jew, but to extend freedom to the slaves and equality to the women was as difficult at that time as it is at present. . . . They experienced the liberation from pagan superstition and the fear of Gods and demons—things for which the people in this area were notorious. . . . Also, throwing off social prejudices and acquiring a 'liberated' way of life must have added to their self-consciousness and self-confidence." [1]

There is a further great miracle in the Galatians' experience. Betz notes that Paul demonstrates "that the Galatians' experience of salvation has happened outside of normal expectation, but that this role of the outsider has always been the trademark of Christianity. The opponents are doubtless correct: what happened to the Galatians should never have happened. Yet it did happen. The same is true of the Christian faith as such. . . The role of the 'outsider' and the appearance of 'illegitimacy' has always been the mark of Christianity. It is the way God works in history." [2] Thus Paul's frequent description of the Christian's life as a "new creation."

RECEIVING THE SPIRIT
• Read the passages in Acts for examples of how the Holy Spirit worked in the early church. What happened in these passages? What does it tell you about the activity of the Spirit?
• Examine the quote by Betz about what it meant for the Galatians to be liberated. From what were they freed? What did that mean, in practical terms?
• From what do you need to be freed and what would that mean in practical terms to you?
• What do you think about a mark of Christianity being its "outsider" status? Do you think that distinction still holds? If not, should the church work to reclaim it? What would that mean? Explain.

Called to Save Sinners

Recall the people whom Jesus called: not the righteous, but the sinners. Paul elaborates this point in Romans 5:6-11. While we were weak, Christ died for us. "God proves his love for us in that while we still were sinners Christ died for us" (Romans 5:8)—while we were God's enemies (Romans 5:10). This designation includes both Jews, who had sinned via transgressions of the law, and "Gentile sinners" (Galatians 2:15), who stood apart from God's revelation of the law. God brings to life "the things that do not exist" (Romans 4:17) and creates a new people, just as God has chosen the Jews as the "fewest of all peoples" and swears to keep God's covenant forever (Deuteronomy 7:7-9; Hosea 2:21-23).

No wonder Paul declared to these Christians, "You foolish Galatians! Who has bewitched you?" (Galatians 3: 1). They were giving up all that wonderful freedom, victory, and grace in order to be "saved" by rites and works, by religious observances and requirements that had already been rendered unnecessary. They were acting as if God's great miracle of the Spirit could be supplemented by something we do and as if God's love (as great as God can love) could be increased or supplemented by some tiny achievement of ours!

Furthermore, the evidence of God's love is already manifested in the lives of the Galatians through the Spirit and through miracles. Did they earn God's love, manifested in those ways, through works? "Of course not!" says Paul. But we, too, think this way much of the time. We have evidences of God's love in our lives; but in times of crisis or insecurity, we fall back on thinking that we must deserve God's love and work for it. We fall back on our own righteousness, on our own achievements. We fall back on thinking that if we do or promise "X," God will be more pleased with us and will move to help us. This is foolish thinking!

Paul uses another word play here. To be "bewitched" means to fall victim of an "evil eye." Paul asks them, in effect, "Who put the evil eye on you and cursed you?" But before the eyes of the Galatians was not a witch's curse but the cursed man Jesus, "publicly exhibited as crucified!" (Galatians 3:1). The death of Jesus was a horrible, public, and humiliating death. Think of the worst shame of which you are most afraid, and know that Jesus suffered a still worse shame. Unclothed, beaten bloody, and abandoned by nearly all his friends, Jesus hung in shame on the cross for agonizing hours as the crowds ridiculed him. But by this "public exhibition" God made a kind of announcement: that salvation is through Christ, that human beings can do nothing and need do nothing to earn God's love; for that love is already theirs.

CALLED TO SAVE SINNERS

- Read Romans 5:6-11 and Galatians 3:1-5. Paul reminds us of human nature: Some of us would be willing to make a sacrifice for someone whom we thought worthy but wouldn't much be bothered for someone we thought wasn't. Who are the most "unworthy" of our society and why? What does it mean to you that Christ died for them? When we think ourselves better, does that then mean that we are more worthy of God's sacrifice?
- In what ways have you already witnessed the gifts of the Spirit? Does this demonstrate to you that you are already one of "God's people"? Explain.

In the Flesh

Jesus' body perished, but he ushered in a distinctly spiritual event. Thus, Paul challenged the Galatians, "Having started with the Spirit, are you now ending with the flesh?" (Galatians 3:3). Paul uses two terms here and also in Romans. The Greek word *sarx* is usually translated "flesh" (as in the word *sarcoma*, cancer of the skin and muscle tissue). But "flesh" is a metaphor for our human existence, not specifically our skin and muscles or, colloquially, our sexuality. We have a physical nature and an inner, psychological nature; and they function together for good and for evil. Furthermore, Paul uses the term to keep before the Galatians his argument about circumcision and the law.

"We know that the law is spiritual," says Paul in Romans 7:14, "but I am of the flesh, sold into slavery under sin." Paul further says, in Romans 8:5-11, that "those who live according to the flesh set their minds on the things of the flesh," which results in death. But when the Spirit dwells within us, we find life and peace. "The mind that is set on the flesh is hostile to God; it does not submit to God's law—indeed it cannot, and those who are in the flesh cannot please God."

These are difficult, somewhat abstract concepts to consider. Isn't our "flesh" (our physical and psychological nature) the place in which God's Spirit dwells? Our "natural" existence has many good aspects, after all. We love one another, we go about our daily work, we look one another in the eyes, we use our minds and our bodies and our femininity or masculinity in positive ways. In other words, we are never "disembodied" people, living only at the level of spirit and soul or only at the level of the carnal with no spirit or soul.

But, of course, our natural existence as "flesh" is also the place where sin lodges itself. Not only our bodies but also (and perhaps especially) our minds and emotions go in many directions. Paul also understood that we are whole people of flesh and spirit together. While being clear about our sinful nature, he affirmed that this life of flesh can "live by faith in the Son of God" (2:20).

IN THE FLESH

• Paul may also mix his metaphors on occasion, or use more than one image that he describes as "flesh." How do you understand the distinction between flesh and spirit?

• Considering the ways in which the Spirit manifested itself in New Testament times, must experiences of the Spirit be "big" events today (such as speaking in tongues, being healed of diseases, and so forth)?

• What have been your personal experiences of God's Spirit? What happened? What was the context?

• If God chooses the "little people" of life, the rejected people at the "edges" of life, who are the people God is seeking today? How are God's followers discovered today?

The Righteous Shall Live by Faith
Read Galatians 3:6-24

Paul begins a section of scriptural proof of the gospel. Read some sections about Abraham in the Old Testament:

- Abraham (Abram) and his extended family came from Ur in the land of the Chaldeans (Genesis 11:27-32).
- God called the seventy-five-year-old Abram to go to the land of Canaan, where God would make of him a great nation. Meanwhile, Abram sojourned in Egypt, where he fibbed and got in trouble with Pharaoh (Genesis 12).
- Abram and his nephew Lot separated, although they still had associations (Genesis 13–14).
- God reaffirmed the covenant with Abram and promised him many descendants (Genesis 15).
- After ten years, Abram and Sarai still had no children; and Abram had a son (Ishmael) by his wife's Egyptian maid, Hagar (Genesis 16).
- God restated the covenant with the ninety-nine-year-old Abram; changed his name to Abraham; and inaugurated the sign of the covenant, circumcision. Both Abraham and Sarah laughed at the thought of having a child at their age (Genesis 17; 18:9-15).
- Abraham entertained heavenly visitors, who eventually brought about the destruction of Sodom and Gomorrah (Genesis 18–19).
- Abraham and Sarah again lied about their relationship, this time to Abimelech of the region of the Negeb. At about the same time, God helped Hagar and Ishmael, whom Sarah drove away (Genesis 20–21).

• After Isaac was born and grew up, God tested Abraham with the near-sacrifice of Isaac (Genesis 22).

These are a few stories about Abraham found in Genesis. Abraham was by no means a perfect person or as perfect in his faith and trust as one might believe if one only read Paul's description. But perhaps having faith in God does not mean perfectly trusting God at every moment, which is difficult, if not impossible, this side of heaven. Abraham, however, knew God's voice and responded when called (Genesis 22:1). He also showed a laudable compassion for people, a deep desire to intercede for people in prayer even though they were guilty of grave sins (Genesis 18:22-33). (How many of us do that as we listen to the evening news, for instance? How many of us, instead, think the guilty should "get what they deserve"?)

In this section of Galatians, Paul argues that the covenant came first because of Abraham's faith. Abraham believed in God's call, "and it was reckoned to him as righteousness" (Galatians 3:6). Through the faith of Abraham, "all the Gentiles shall be blessed" (Galatians 3:8; Genesis 12:3 has "all the families of the earth," which means the same thing).

Paul elaborates this point more fully in Romans 4. Abraham did nothing (He had no "works") to make him justified by God. He simply believed in God's promises. We too, says Paul, need simply to believe, to have faith. Furthermore, Abraham was uncircumcised when God called him. Circumcision came *after* God had accounted him righteous. Circumcision, then, is no requirement one must follow in order to be blessed by God. Abraham "received the sign of circumcision as a seal of the righteousness that he had by faith while he was still uncircumcised. The purpose was to make him the ancestor of all who believe without being circumcised and who thus have righteousness reckoned to them, and likewise the ancestor of the circumcised who are not only circumcised but who also follow the example of the faith that our ancestor Abraham had before he was circumcised" (Romans 4:11-12).

In Galatians, Paul argues that these Scriptures foreshadow the gospel of Christ; for Abraham came 430 years before the giving of the law (Galatians 3:17). Employing the style of biblical exposition typical of the Pharisees, Paul argues from a variety of Scripture. Using a play on one single word (a favorite rabbinical device), Paul states that the covenant between God and Abraham was "to his offspring" (or "seed"; Galatians 3:16). *Offspring* could be a plural or a singular noun. Paul argues that the noun is not plural but singular, "that is, to one person, who is Christ" (Galatians 3:16). Just as no one can change a will once it is legalized, so no one can annul a covenant. The law of God, given so many generations after Abraham, was not an afterthought or a new covenant that abrogated the covenant with Abraham. It was "added because of transgressions, until the offspring ["seed"] would come to whom the promise had been made; and it was ordained through angels by a mediator" (Galatians 3:19).

THE RIGHTEOUS SHALL LIVE BY FAITH

• In small groups, divide the Scripture passages from Genesis and read further in the life of Abraham. What do you learn about Abraham, Sarah, and their covenant with God? How does this shed light on Paul's argument about righteousness and faith?

• Read Galatians 3:6-24. How does Paul in this portion of his letter explain the value and purpose of the law? How is it related to God's covenant with the Hebrews?

• There is value and blessing in participating in the great continuity of the faithful—being a descendant of Abraham, in effect—but we are saved by faith. What would the community of faith be like if only those who attained some level of righteousness first were saved? Would you be saved? How could humans quantify how good "good" would have to be in order to be saved?

Salvation and the Law

For Paul, it is clear that anyone who seeks salvation through the law must keep the whole law (Galatians 3:10; see Leviticus 18:5); and anyone who does not do so is cursed. But the prophets say, "The one who is righteous will live by faith" (Galatians 3:11, quoting Habakkuk 2:4). This in effect proves, says Paul, that we are never justified by works of the law but by faith—just as Abraham was.

This is now possible because "Christ redeemed us from the curse of the law by becoming a curse for us—for it is written, 'Cursed is everyone who hangs on a tree'—in order that in Christ Jesus the blessing of Abraham might come to the Gentiles" (Galatians 3:13-14). The curse is given in Deuteronomy 21:22-23. Christ was cursed under the law because he was executed as a criminal in order that the promise might come to all.

So why was the law given? God gave the law in order to define his will vis-à-vis sin and obedience. Without law, no one would know what is right and wrong. But the law cannot help a person cure sin; that is why we need a mediator and savior.

Verses 19 and 20 of Galatians 3 are difficult to understand, but they seem to refer to rabbinical interpretations of the law and how it was given. Although Exodus 19–20 states that God did give the Law directly to Moses, the ancient rabbis believed that, since God is so holy, God must have needed the mediation of angels to give the Law to human beings: Moses and the people. But while the Law was given through mediators, the Savior came directly from God and indeed was God.

Because salvation came directly from God, the new covenant could not be broken (as could the law, when people sinned). Human sin does not break the covenant because the initiative is wholly on God's side.

Nevertheless, the law is not antithetical to God. Not only did (and does) it define right and wrong, it "imprisoned all things under the power of sin, so that what was promised through faith in Jesus Christ might be given to those who believe" (Galatians 3:22). The law functioned as "disciplinarian" (Galatians 3:24) until Christ came. Now we no longer need its discipline, for we have the guidance of the Spirit (Galatians 3:25-26).

For the faithful Jew, the law functions in a much more positive way: as an expression of God's holy will to follow. Paul came to understand the law in a different way because he accepted the radical notion of Jesus as the Messiah who, according to the Pharisaic interpretation of the law, was cursed for having been "hanged on the tree." For the strict Pharisee, the Messiah could not come to such a fate, nor could the law itself suffer such an offense as to be accused of violating the Messiah. How can Paul, steeped in his Pharisaic tradition *and* converted by the risen Christ, now understand the role of law and faith? He returns to his argument that while the law cannot give life, it can point the way to life in the crucified and resurrected Christ.

SALVATION AND THE LAW

• Paul intensifies his commentary on the law and salvation by introducing the notion of curse. Review Galatians 3:10-14. What does it mean that Jesus "was cursed under the law"? that he "became a curse for us"? How does this "curse" actually bless the believers in Jesus Christ?

• Paul next argues that God's covenant can be breached by the sinfulness of persons, but a covenant given directly through Jesus Christ cannot. Read Galatians 3:15-22. What does Paul suggest about Jesus as the offspring of Abraham? Did the Savior have to be a Jew? That is, did the Savior have to be one of the people descended from Abraham? How is God's promise fulfilled through the covenant initiated by the Christ?

• Read Galatians 3:23-24. The "disciplinarian" in Greek is *paidagogos*, a slave who guarded and supervised children and ensured that they safely attended school. How does the law function as a teacher or a servant that leads us to wisdom?

Children Rather Than Slaves
Read Galatians 3:25–4:7

Get a good discussion going in your church school class concerning Paul and women:

• 1 Corinthians 7:1-2: "Now concerning the matters about which you wrote: 'It is well for a man not to touch a woman.' But because of cases of sexual immorality, each man should have his own wife and each woman her own husband."

• 1 Corinthians 11:3: "But I want you to understand that Christ is the head of every man, and the husband is the head of his wife."

• 1 Corinthians 14:33b-35: "As in all the churches of the saints, women should be silent in the churches. For they are not permitted to speak, but should be subordinate, as

the law also says. If there is anything they desire to know, let them ask their husbands at home."
- 1 Timothy 2:11-15: "Let a woman learn in silence with full submission. I permit no woman to teach or to have authority over a man. . . . Adam was not deceived, but the woman was deceived and became a transgressor. Yet she will be saved through childbearing."

Some scholars question whether Paul authored all these words, arguing that First Timothy is a pseudonymous work and that the First Corinthians passages are later additions. Whether that is true or is not, we find in Galatians that Paul's theology is often better (at least in our modern understanding of gender roles) than his practical advice. [4]

"There is no longer Jew or Greek, there is no longer slave or free, there is no longer male and female; for all of you are one in Christ Jesus" (Galatians 3:28). This beautiful passage affirms that everyone is, together, a child of God through faith. As we have been baptized in Christ, so we are clothed in him (Galatians 3:27). As the early Christians wore a similar kind of garment when baptized, so are all Christians "robed" in Christ's holiness.

The teaching of Galatians 3:28 harks back to the issue of circumcision. It is not just that, in Jewish practice at least (barring the abhorrent practice of female circumcision in some cultures), boys were circumcised and girls were not. Women were certainly included in the covenant. But grace, whether understood in an "Old Testament" or in a "New Testament" kind of way, overcomes all divisions, all barriers, and all levels. (Reread Ephesians 2, for instance.) In God's grace all people are unified and made equal.

The words *Jew* and *Greek* (which mean Jew and Gentile) are both ethnic and religious in meaning. One can change religion, but one cannot change one's ethnic background. Although there is such a thing as transgendered people, typically one does not and cannot change one's gender. In the ancient world, slavery was an accepted though abhorrent practice; even the Torah stipulates the treatment of slaves and provides various legalities (Genesis 29:24; Exodus 21:2-11, 26-27; Leviticus 25:39; 44; Deuteronomy 15:12-13). These human distinctions are, on one level, not abrogated. Paul himself lived within the world in which these distinctions were found and, in some ways, did not think it necessary to criticize the injustices inherent in human relations. After all, he believed Christ was coming very soon; he would have seen no need to "change the world" by attacking the institution of slavery, for instance.

But in Christ one finds equality as God's children. God has adopted us as precious heirs, "heirs according to the promise" (Galatians 3:29). This was the wonderful message that Paul wanted to impress on the Galatians.

CHILDREN RATHER THAN SLAVES

• Read Galatians 3:25-26. Now that Christ has come, is there any longer a need for the *paidogogos*—something outside of Christ that leads us to wisdom? Explain.

• Read Galatians 3:27-29. What does Paul mean that now all are one in Christ? How would you describe these distinctions? Are they literal, do you think, or metaphorical? How would you paraphrase this passage to make it speak specifically to your culture and location? Is this passage liberating to you personally? Explain what it means to your own faith and life.

• Is baptism necessary for salvation? Some Christian denominations respond with an unequivocal "yes" and believe that baptism has to be performed in a certain way (submersion, sprinkling, and so forth). Do Paul's teachings about circumcision imply that nothing, not even baptism, is required for salvation? Or is baptism a necessary part of the new covenant?

• Argue these positions: (1) Christians should try to save people's souls rather than to address social problems. (2) Christians should address injustices as they arise in society (sexism, racism, ecological issues, and so forth). (3) Christians should try to balance evangelism and social action.

• Read Galatians 4:1-7. What does it mean to be a child rather than a slave? In early America the message of Christ gave a sense of identity to slaves who found freedom and dignity in the gospel that they could not find in society. But this spiritual freedom eventually led them to social freedom as well. How do we find a new identity as God's children? What changes happen in our lives because of our new identity?

IN CLOSING

• Summarize your learning from this chapter. How is the image of law and freedom and law and salvation coming together for you?

• Close with prayer for those who are still marginalized by society and who are not considered as persons of worth. Pray for freedom and peace for all of God's children.

---

[1] From *Galatians*, by Hans Dieter Betz (Fortress Press, 1979); page 3.

[2] From *Galatians*; pages 30–31.

[3] From *The Letters to the Galatians and Ephesians*, by William Barclay (Westminster Press, 1976); page 31.

[4] See also *Paul and the Corinthians*, by Robert Wingard (Abingdon Press, 1999) for a more thorough treatment of Paul's teaching and attitude about women.

V WHAT IS LIBERTY?

"Abba! Father!"
Read Galatians 4:1-11

My father passed away during the time I was writing this lesson. I thought how, at the time of death, we rely on the grace of God in a particularly important way. If we are the ones facing death, we can look to God with confidence in salvation. That is the time we may think, *What if I'm not good enough to be saved? Why couldn't I have done "X" in order to ensure God's salvation?* These are deeply frightening thoughts—thoughts that completely miss the point of the gospel. If we have faith in Christ, we have no need of that kind of wrong-headed thinking. God has done everything; Christ has prepared a place for us in his Father's house that has many dwelling places (John 14:1-14). This passage from John never states that Christ will prepare a place for us in his Father's house only if we provide a certain amount of lumber and dry wall for the job! The Letter to the Galatians assures us that is not the case. If we are the ones who are bereaved, we similarly can look to God with confidence that he loves us and stoops to help us.

As I worked on legal and insurance matters with my mother (with that numb yet overwhelmed feeling one has amid a recent death), I thought of this passage in

Galatians (4:1-7). At age forty-two, I am not a minor; but my father and mother have kept certain things in trust for me and for my daughter, their only granddaughter—our family's ancestral farm, for instance—until a future time when I might inherit. When one is an heir, often one has holdings that are put in trust until one is a certain age or until one's parents are gone. Continuing his analogy of the law as our caretaker until the time of Christ, Paul declares the obvious for the sake of the main point: We have a different legal and social status as children than we have when we are adults.

Many of us are familiar with the Jewish pattern. When boys and girls are thirteen, they each go through a very beautiful and affirming ceremony of adulthood. This is a lovely occasion that I have had the pleasure of attending. For a boy this is called a "bar mitzvah" (which means "son of the commandment"), for he is now old enough to keep God's commandments and to make moral decisions. For a girl this is called a "bat mitzvah" ("daughter of the commandment"). One is truly blessed when one is "of age" and can keep God's will.

Customs differed in the ancient world. In the Roman Empire a boy became an adult during what we call adolescence and participated in a festival called the *Liberalia*. Often a girl or boy presented a toy (like a doll or a ball) to the god Apollo as a symbol that she or he had left childhood for adulthood. In ancient Greece a boy became an adult at eighteen, and his long hair was cut and offered as a sacrifice to the deity. Thus adulthood occurred at a specific time. Paul's point may seem clear at first. The law served us until the time that Christ came and we were adopted as God's children.

"ABBA! FATHER!"

• Think of anything of yours that is entrusted to your children, to your grandchildren, or to someone else. What possession of yours do you most want to pass along to the next generation? What about that possession makes it so special?

• Read Galatians 4:1-7. How would you put into your own words the relationship Paul describes between humankind and God? Is this the way you think of your own relationship with God? How is it similar or different?

• If you had a limited time to live, what would you do? How confident would you be in prayer? How does Paul's message—that we are saved wholly by grace and never of ourselves—change your thinking?

• Do you have adoptive children, or were you adopted? Discuss adoption in our modern society. How does our understanding of adoption help our understanding of Paul's letter to the Galatians?

Elemental Spirits

Paul continued his line of reasoning about the relationship to God by introducing an interesting if ambiguous word. When we were minors, he says, we were enslaved to *stoicheia*. This word may mean "elemental spirits of the world," as explained in Galatians 4:3, 8, which are "beings that by nature are not gods." In other words, we were enslaved to cosmic forces, which the Galatians would have understood in the context of the polytheism and mystical religions of Greek and Roman society.

Or the word may mean the four basic elements of the world: earth, fire, air, and water. Thus we were enslaved to the world as natural beings ("flesh") therein. Or the word can mean "elementary knowledge," such as religious practices and basic religious knowledge, "special days, and months, and seasons, and years" (Galatians 4:10).

The Jewish Torah is not exactly "elementary knowledge" to a Jew but rather deeply meaningful and deeply symbolic and multifaceted Scripture. It is not entirely clear if Paul is calling the law *stoicheia* or if he is speaking more generally of elemental spirits (like the "angels," "rulers," and "powers" that cannot separate us from God's love according to Romans 8:38). Paul's basic point is that the Galatians have been set free! They are no longer slaves to anything but have "received adoption as children" (Galatians 4:5). They are known by God and know God, so why should they fall back on older spirits and older observances that are now irrelevant to them (Galatians 4:9)? Why do they listen to teachers who demand that they be circumcised in order to be saved?

Paul is so perplexed with them that he declares, "I am afraid that my work for you may have been wasted" (Galatians 4:11). He does not lament that his time was wasted—Paul never speaks of wasted time in his letters—but that the Galatians were losing the most important thing they could ever have: the good news of Christ. That good news means a personal relationship with God who does not demand observances but instead wants us as trusting, obedient children.

ELEMENTAL SPIRITS

• Read Galatians 4:8-11. Explore the term *stoicheia* and what it might mean. How would you paraphrase this passage? Remember that the Galatians were considered "barbarians" and came from a polytheistic background. How might they interpret this passage?

• How do you know you have the Spirit? How do you address God in prayer? With fear? With confidence? With trust? With anxiety?

• How does Paul fear that this conflict between observance (for the sake of observance or ritual only) and obedience (and care) as loved children will play out for the Galatians? What might be some concrete examples of Paul's "work being wasted"? Taking his fears and claims to heart today, how might we describe the danger and the opportunity that Paul wrote about and apply it to ourselves or to the church?

Come to Papa

Though Paul expressed his concern, the Galatians can still cry to God in a gentle, trusting way, "Abba! Father!" One of my students at the Louisville Seminary said that when she visited a synagogue with her church group, the rabbi's little child came running up calling, "Abba! Abba!" The incident illustrated how we might relate to God in childlike love. *Abba* is the Aramaic, diminutive word for "Father," a word that we could use for God (Mark 14:36; Romans 8:15). Paul, too, said that we can call God "Abba" by the Spirit of God; so we know thereby we are not slaves but God's children through Jesus Christ (Romans 8:15-16).

Our relationships to our earthly parents may encourage or preclude such affectionate terminology. Perhaps the word *Mommy* serves better than the word *Daddy* to communicate our closeness to God; or perhaps the word *Daddy* serves just fine. Maybe our earthly parents were such that we have to relearn how to approach God with childlike love; in fact, efforts to relearn God's love and heal from traumas or parental disappointments in our family of origin sometimes characterize (or propel) our spiritual journeys. But as the Spirit comes to us, we understand afresh what kind of relationship we can have with God who invites us and desires for us to call out to our divine "Daddy!" or "Mommy!" in a happy, trusting, and close relationship.

COME TO PAPA

• Do you ever think about God as "Daddy"? as "Mommy"? How has your own image and experience of the parental role modeled for you or influenced your image and experience of a God we call Father

(or Mother)? If you are a parent, are you mindful of the ways your parenting might influence your child's concept of God as parent? What difference does that potential influence make in what you do and say?
• Review the two Scriptures that refer to God as "Abba." What does knowing that Jesus or other faithful ancestors regarded God as "Daddy" say to you about God? about how others related to God? about how you can relate to God?

Paul's Experience
Read Galatians 4:12-31

As stated earlier, Paul does not mention the location from which he wrote the Letter to the Galatians. He also does not include his travel plans—an important aspect of some other letters (for instance, Romans 15:22-29 and 1 Corinthians 16:5-9). He does, however, say that he wishes he could travel again to Galatia as he recalls his positive treatment during an earlier visit (Galatians 4:13-14). Paul alludes to some kind of physical illness that had, apparently, caused him to tarry in Galatia. This became the occasion for his preaching to them, but the Book of Acts does not mention a sojourn in Galatia in order for Paul to recuperate. This visit could have been the visit mentioned in the Acts 13–14 material or the quick trip through Asia Minor in Acts 16 (see Chapter 1, pages 19–22, for a review of the geography of the area) or some other time that Acts does not mention.

The Galatians not only accepted Paul and the gospel in spite of his apparently difficult illness but also welcomed him "as an angel of God," as indeed Christ himself (Galatians 4:14). "Had it been possible, you would have torn out your eyes and given them to me" (Galatians 4:15), he writes. This statement makes us wonder if Paul had some kind of eye problem like an infection. Whatever Paul's condition was, it must have been repulsive or difficult for others to tolerate. Was this his "thorn in the flesh" to which he alludes in 2 Corinthians 12:7-9, an illness (if the "thorn" was indeed an illness) that some have speculated was malaria or epilepsy?

We do not know, but we do know that Paul and the Galatians became very close at that time. If you have some painful illness (I sometimes have migraine headaches; my mother has rheumatoid arthritis.), you know about suffering. You also know how much it means when someone is caring and understanding toward you when you are in pain, not impatient and condescending. Paul felt genuinely grateful for the hospitality he received from the Galatians. We should read the Letter to the Galatians as frustrated words to people Paul cared about deeply. He would have gladly suffered for them in return (Galatians 4:19-20).

Hospitality was an important virtue (Romans 12:13). Abraham showed hospitality to the Lord's angels (Genesis 18:1-8). Lot actually put his family's safety behind his desire to be a protective host to the two guests (God's angels) whom the crowds of Sodom demanded (Genesis 19:1-11). The Torah has commands to care for strangers, too (Leviticus 19:33-34). The Letter to the Galatians also reflects the importance of this virtue.

So Paul was perplexed. He asks, "Have I now become your enemy by telling you the truth?" (Galatians 4:16). Sometimes, to use a cliché, the truth hurts. We all have been in situations wherein we did not want to hear the truth or to level with someone else. Yet the truth Paul speaks is not a hard, difficult one. Jesus' yoke is easy, and his burden is light (Matthew 11:28-30). The teachers in

Galatia, in contrast, flattered the church in an attempt to persuade the Galatians to take on the burdens of circumcision and extra rites (Galatians 4:17).

PAUL'S EXPERIENCE

• Read Galatians 4:12-20, and recall Paul's concern about the "elemental spirits." What then does he mean by saying that the Galatians should become as he is and he has become as they are? (See also 1 Corinthians 11:1 and 9:19-23.)

• Paul's goal is to restore and rectify his relationship with the Galatians. How does his tone change? What appeals does he make? What personal references? What, do you think, was the effect of these appeals? What concerns does he still have?

• Look up the references to hospitality in Romans and Genesis and research hospitality in a Bible dictionary. How is the biblical notion of hospitality like your current understanding? How is it different? Have you ever suffered for the sake of hospitality (and we don't mean the superficial suffering of putting up with a bore or a badly cooked meal) or for the sake of the truth? Describe that experience and what you learned from it.

• Many of us are familiar with the expression "entertaining angels unawares," which comes from the King James Version of Hebrews 13:2. Have you ever given help to someone in a particularly special way? If so, what were the circumstances?

• How do we discover God in the midst of great pain (whether emotional or physical)?

A Complicated Allegory

Paul uses an allegorical illustration to make his point about the interrelationship of law and freedom. Read Genesis 16 and 21:1-21. Since Abram and Sarai still had no children nearly eleven years after God's initial promise, Sarai suggested that her barrenness must have a divine cause. So she thought Abram should have a child by her maid Hagar. Unfortunately (in this very human story!),

Sarai became fiercely jealous of Hagar once the latter had become pregnant; and Abram gave in to his wife's demands (Genesis 16:1-6). Fortunately, the Lord blessed Hagar in her distress and promised her many descendants. She was told to name the child Ishmael, which means "God hears." Years later Hagar again faced Sarah's mean-spiritedness, and Abraham weakly sent Hagar and Ishmael away. Once more the Lord promised to be with the rejected mother and son and subsequently blessed them.

Paul goes on to compare Hagar with Sarah ("a free woman" in Galatians 4:22 and "the other woman" in 4:26) in a complicated allegory. Some of Paul's illustrations are obtuse or inconsistent. He is usually sufficiently clear in his discussions (though not always). This is one of the inadequate illustrations, however. Paul says that this story represents two covenants. Abraham had two sons, one by a slave woman, Hagar, and one by his wife, Sarah, who was free. The slave's child was "born according to the flesh" (Galatians 4:23), and the other child was "born through the promise." Hagar, he says, represents Mount Sinai and children bound for slavery and the earthly Jerusalem. Sarah represents the heavenly Jerusalem and the freedom of persons under the new covenant. As Hagar and Ishmael were driven away, so must the slavery of the law so that we might be free in Christ (Galatians 4:30–5:1).

The illustration contains inconsistencies. The covenant of Mount Sinai was not a "fleshly" afterthought. Mount Sinai belongs to the promises of God beginning with the promise to Abraham for a child, Isaac, as Paul has stated (Romans 3:1-4; Galatians 3:18). In addition, Sinai was one sacred place to which the Hebrews headed on their departure from slavery and is the site of the giving of the Law. Likewise, the city of Jerusalem was a central place both in

the hearts of the Jews from the time of David's kingship
and throughout the life of Jesus and in the hearts of
Christians to the present. The Gentile Galatians may not
have been particularly moved by the importance of either
place in the covenants that were foreign to their own pre-
vious religious experience.

Referring again to the inconsistencies of this argument,
it should be noted that God also blessed both Hagar and
Sarah with many descendants. But this is a typical kind of
allegorical biblical exposition that Pharisees like Paul
enjoyed and employed; and it is consistent with his point
that the law defined transgressions which, in turn, placed
us in bondage to sin. In Galatians, Paul uses this story to
reiterate once again his major point: "For freedom Christ
has set us free" (Galatians 5:1).

A COMPLICATED ALLEGORY

• Read Galatians 4:21-31 and the passages from Genesis 16 and 21.
Refresh your thinking about the relationship between Hagar and Sarah
and between Abraham and these two mothers of his sons. Keeping in
mind that the analogy is not exact, what is Paul's point about the two
covenants?
• When we are "set free" by Christ, what makes our lives different from
before? What is "driven out"? What is retained? How are we "set free"
for "freedom"?

Threats to Liberty
Read Galatians 5:1-15

Scholars use the term *paraenesis* to describe the form of
ancient letters that included exhortations, commands, or
general ethical instruction. In Romans, for instance, this
material is found in 12:1–15:32. In First Corinthians, it is

found in most of the letter (5:1–16:18). In Galatians, Paul gives the churches instructions in the section 5:1–6:15, although he has given instruction throughout the letter and his specific ethical recommendations begin with Galatians 5:13.

Circumcision is of no use to the Galatians. Paul has already made that point clear, but he reiterates it (Galatians 5:2-3). He puts it in very strong terms: Christ will be useless to you if you are circumcised; and again, if you are circumcised, you will have to keep the whole law and forget about Christ having any benefit. Keeping the whole law is a never-ending process; you are "locked in" for the rest of your life. In Christ, you have been set free. In fact, Christ has set us free so that we might have freedom for service to him and to one another. Because we have this precious freedom, we do not need to fear that we cannot do enough for Christ because Christ has already done everything for us. In Christ, what counts is "faith working through love," not circumcision or its absence (Galatians 5:6).

One senses that Paul is making light of the religious naivete of the Galatians. To think that one small rite would make a person forsake the whole gospel!

Consider the phrase "fallen away from grace" (Galatians 5:4). What does that phrase usually mean? Usually it means some kind of moral lapse. Interestingly, Paul employs the phrase to refer to the Galatians' supposed religious conscientiousness! They want to be obedient, so they allow circumcision. They want to keep the law and also to hold to Christ. One can "fall away from grace" through excessive religious devotion as well as through moral lapse if one forgets that salvation is of God alone and never of us.

Continuing his argument, Paul reasons that if circumcision is still necessary, then he is being persecuted for no particular reason (Galatians 5:11). Much of the persecution aimed at Paul came from Jews. Tragically, Jews have been victims of persecution from Christians, a shameful racism by those who revere a Jewish Jesus as Savior. So we must be careful to understand the context in which Paul wrote: as a Jew embroiled in controversy with other Jews.

Paul puts his frustration strongly: "I wish those [the Judaizers] who unsettle you would castrate themselves!" (Galatians 5:12). If the circumcision teachers at Galatia believe that genital surgery is necessary for salvation, why do they not just remove their genitals entirely? The Galatians would have known that some Greek worshipers of the goddess Cybele mutilated themselves by castration as part of their religious devotion; so Paul may be likening the Galatians to those "heathen" priests who have nothing to do with Christianity, although to compare them or the Judaizers to this cult would be thoroughly insulting. He is also making a word play between the Greek words "cutting off" (translated as "castrate" in verse 12) and "cutting in" in verse 7, which can be translated, "You were running well; who cut in on your (running)?"

One of the key passages of the letter is 5:13-15. We are called to freedom, but freedom does not mean self-indulgence (or obeying the flesh). It means, paradoxically, becoming slaves to one another through Christian love according to the commandment (which summarizes the whole law), " 'You shall love your neighbor as yourself.' If, however, you bite and devour one another, take care that you are not consumed by one another."

The church should be the place where we are "slaves to

one another" (Galatians 5:13). The church should be the place where people find caring and healing. (See the next lesson.) But sometimes churches are very human, hurtful places. Some churches contain factions and in-groups, parishioners who want to run things and who create conflict when they cannot. Some churches contain people who are searching for something in their lives but react angrily when they cannot find that unarticulated, disquieting "something." Sometimes people are even harassed and abused in church settings. I speak in general here, but truly Paul is correct. If we mistreat one another, we take grave risks with one another and hold up Christ to contempt. Paul reminds us that the church exists for one thing: for love of God and love of neighbor. It is a great blessing when we have such a church in our lives.

THREATS TO LIBERTY

• Read Galatians 5:1-15. Paul summarizes his argument about the need for circumcision. Why is he so opposed to it for the Galatians? What does this rite or ritual represent to him, in the context of the Galatian church? What rituals do we follow today in the church that now seem to be irrelevant? How do we decide when a rite or ritual has "outlived its usefulness" or may in fact do more harm than good? How do we confront the need to change?

• Refer again to Galatians 5:13-15. What does the term *Christian freedom* mean to you? How do you understand the paradox of having freedom by being a slave or servant for Christ?

• How is your church serving others in Christian love? How is it falling short? Does service mean adding new programs (and finding volunteers) or developing a sense of calling, cooperation, and love or both? Explain.

IN CLOSING

• Summarize your learnings on liberty and the law. Join together in prayer for understanding the liberty we have in Christ.

VI LIFE IN THE SPIRIT

The Life of Liberty
Read Galatians 5:16-26

S everal years ago an interview of Christian novelist Reynolds Price appeared in the literary journal *The Georgia Review*. Price said at one point, "It's the great thing that institutional Christianity constantly fails to do— that is, to remember Jesus' saying, 'Do unto others,' or when God says, 'I will have mercy and not sacrifice,' or " 'Vengeance is mine,' "sayeth the Lord," 'I will repay.' " Christian churches seem to be too busy getting vengeance on and sacrificing other Christians, not with mercy and forgiveness."[1] The interviewer interjected, "William Faulkner said, 'The trouble with Christianity is we haven't tried it yet.' "[2]

Do you agree with that statement? The opinion may be applied too broadly, although some churches and some Christians certainly do forget the mercy to which God calls us. To paraphrase the apostle James in his letter, our mouths are excellent barometers for the state of our souls. (We can fool ourselves in our minds, but our mouths give us away.) How loving are we in the judgments we pass on one another? How angry and judgmental do we become toward individuals we know, toward our public officials and leaders? Can we think of anyone we have hurt by our words and our actions?

Ironically, we stumble as Christians in this way—not so much because we forget the "rules" of the faith, but because we give up our freedom. Christ has set us free to be free (Galatians 5:1), and that freedom means doing all the good we can as we are guided by the Holy Spirit. Yet we continually slip back into bondage—to the law, to our old natures. My pastor here in Kentucky recently preached a sermon about "Back to Egypt" committees. Drawing on the Old Testament stories of Moses and the Israelites, he talked about the desire to stick with the familiar, even if the familiar is Egyptian slavery! Our churches sometimes do this. They long for the "good old days" rather than envisioning new possibilities. Individuals do this, too, on occasion. We find it scarier to trust God wholly than to reserve some area of our lives for our control. Paul sees the Galatians succumbing to old ways rather than living as free people in Christ.

"Live by the Spirit," says Paul, "and do not gratify the desires of the flesh" (Galatians 5:16). Again, we may be misled by the way the word *sarx* is translated as "flesh." Paul is not saying, "Live by the Spirit, and do not go out and eat and drink too much and have lots of immoral sex," although those things are included in his list of "works of the flesh." About half the vices Paul lists in Galatians 5:19-21 have to do with attitudes and relation-ships—the "little" sins that we think are "all right" compared to the "big" sins. But living by the Spirit means excluding the "scandalous" sins like immorality and drunkenness and also exclusion of the "respectable" sins like envy, telling people off, rushing into conflict, judging others, and so forth.

The Works of the Flesh

How does the Spirit guide us if we do not have "the law" to tell us what we should do? As Hans Deiter Betz puts it, Paul sees good and evil as opposing forces working in our lives. When the good (that is, the Holy Spirit) comes into an individual or into a Christian community, the Spirit "fills" the person or the group so that the evil (the "works of the flesh") is pushed out. There is no room for the works of the flesh because the Spirit is working. That is how we can produce "the fruit of the Spirit" without worrying about following certain rules and laws to produce this "fruit." [3]

As Calvin Roetzel puts it, there are three kinds of ethical instructions in Paul's letters. One is the string of moral maxims (for instance, Romans 12:9-13) that are only generally related to one another. Another is the homily that addresses particular situations and issues (for instance, 1 Corinthians 5–15). The third kind is the catalog of vices and virtues—again, only generally and vaguely interrelated—that we find in Galatians 5:19-23. The vices and virtues are not necessarily Jewish in origin (although they are consistent with Jewish morality) because Greek writings often mention these very sins and virtues. As Roetzel points out, however, Paul innovates by making these virtues "the fruit of the Spirit," connecting them thereby with the Jewish and Christian traditions. [4]

"The works of the flesh [of our natural, nonspiritual existence] are obvious" (Galatians 5:19). Take a moment to consider these works:

- **Fornication.** The Greek word is *porneia*, from which we get the word *pornography*. *Porneia* can mean prostitution but also any sexual practice that violates the marital relationship and, in turn, one's relationship to Christ. Our modern world tolerates extramarital sex, and so did Paul's world (as seen in 1 Corinthians 6:13-20; 10:1-13).
- **Impurity.** The word is *akatharsia*, which can mean ancient taboos against corpses, lepers, and so forth that were supposed to bring spiritual defilement to persons. But the word more broadly means that which defiles one's faith.
- **Licentiousness.** *Aselgeia* means lewdness or wantonness or willfulness.
- **Idolatry.** This is a word for something that Jews and Christians alike (and Muslims, too) considered a fundamental sin, that is, the elevation of something above God in one's worship and loyalties, whether a literal or a figurative idol. (Muslims know that anything, even fear, can become an idol because that fear becomes first in one's thinking rather than God.)
- **Sorcery**, or witchcraft, refers to the use of drugs, usually in connection with magic.
- **Enmities**, or hatred, directed at God or at one's fellow human beings.

- **Strife**, which is hostility or rivalry, discord, and contention.
- **Jealousy**. *Zelos*, from which we get the English word *zeal*, can be a good or a bad thing, a healthy and strong devotion or a greedy and selfish kind of zeal.
- **Anger**, or wrath, an explosive temper.
- **Quarrels**, or better, selfishness or strife as in the older translations.
- **Dissensions**, which is closer to the meaning of quarrels.
- **Factions**, which is translated *heresies* and *party spirit* in older translations. The Greek word *haireseis* (or heresy) essentially means choice or freedom but negatively can mean rivalries over matters of recognition in the church.
- **Envy**, or ill will, which was one of the first human sins — of Cain.
- **Drunkenness**, the habitual misuse of intoxicants that was common in the Greek world.
- **Carousing**, which is related to drunkenness.

"I am warning you," says Paul, "those who do such things will not inherit the kingdom of God" (Galatians 5:21). There is, of course, only one sin that is unforgivable, according to Jesus. The only unforgivable sin is the continual, persistent, deliberate, and contentious resistance to the Holy Spirit's power and testimony (Matthew 12:31-32; Mark 3:29). Thank the Lord that he forgives us and remakes us as we fall and return. As John Wesley reminds us, "prevenient grace" works in the lives of even the most offensive sinner so that persons may hopefully someday come to repentance. But those who allow the "work of the flesh" to take pride of place in their lives must be careful lest they miss God's presence and work in their lives.

THE WORKS OF THE FLESH

• Greek thought allowed for the segmentation of mind and body and thus permitted licentiousness (Only the spirit matters; the body is of no account, so I can do as I please.). Jewish thought could not separate the two (I am a whole person called to devote heart, mind, soul, and strength to God.). Paul recognized the internal tug of war fueled by sin and moderated against by good, or the Spirit. Read Galatians 5:16-21. How do you understand the distinction between Spirit and flesh?

• Review this long list of vices in the text and in the Bible. Discuss the definitions as they would have been understood by Paul and the Galatians.

• Some of these vices are very serious; some feel more like "garden variety" or "little" sins that we can't help but engage in. (What human being doesn't experience envy or strife once in a while?) In the faith context, is there any such thing as a "big" or a "small" sin?

• If you feel comfortable in your group, consider which of these vices is most troublesome to you. What can you do, perhaps with the support of Christian friends, to begin to overcome that sin?

• How do you understand the "unforgivable sin"?

The Fruits of the Spirit

There is, of course, good news. Paul lists the fruit of the Spirit:

• **Love**, or *agape*, the love of God that redeems *eros*, or human love, so that mutuality and devotion are present among believers.

• **Joy**, or *chara*, which is related to the Greek word for grace, *charis*.

• **Peace**, or *eirene*, which is related to the Hebrew word *shalom* as meaning wholeness and well-being.

• **Patience**, which is a strong kind of patience rather than a general pleasant nature.

• **Kindness**, or gentleness, as in, "Love is patient; love is kind" (1 Corinthians 13:4). Kindness included charac-

teristics of goodness and character as well as compassion
and patience.

- **Generosity,** *agathosune,* which means the characteristics
of righteousness and goodness.
- **Faithfulness,** or *pistis,* which means both faith and trust-
worthiness.
- **Gentleness,** or meekness, the characteristic of people
who will inherit the earth according to the Beatitudes. It
is submissiveness to God's will as well as consideration.
- **Self-control,** a Greek virtue that means self-mastery and
integrity.

Reread John 15:17. Jesus tells his disciples, "I am giving you these commands so that you may love one another."
That word *may* is important. Jesus does not say, "You
should love one another," or "You have to love one another."
The word *may* indicates that permission to love is being
given and also implies the power to love that is granted to
us. That is the work of the Spirit. That is Paul's confident
foundation for Christian ethics and mutuality.

The vices listed here in Galatians can be controlled by
rites and rules; but if the heart is unclean, the law has not
really done the job of transforming a person. Jewish writ-
ers speak of training a person's intentions: guiding a person toward a transformation of the heart; so, too, Paul's
teachings here in Galatians. None of these fruits of the
Spirit can be controlled by rites and rules. They spring
from the Spirit's work within us.

THE FRUITS OF THE SPIRIT

- Read Galatians 5:22-26. Review these definitions as Paul and the
Galatians would have understood them. Are any of these "fruits" different from what you thought? If so, how?

• As with the vices, is it possible to quantify or prioritize these spiritual traits and behaviors? Is it better, for example, to be loving than to be patient?

• Often we glorify action heroes who conquer through power, and we also glorify Jesus and Paul who teach a different kind of power. How are the comparatively gentle fruits of the Spirit ways in which we have power? Is this power consistent with the virtues we associate with powerful people?

• In what ways does the Spirit show us ourselves? How does God train us amid our everyday lives? What are some situations and events in which God trains you to have the fruit of the Spirit? What are some other ways?

• Take a personal inventory, either alone or with one other person whom you trust. How mature are these fruits in you? Do you feel God drawing you to greater faithfulness in any of these traits? Which ones are the most difficult for you? How can you, with the support of Christian friends, cultivate these spiritual traits and disciplines?

Liberty Together
Read Galatians 6:1-10

We have in Galatians 6:1-6 a remarkable portrait of Christian fellowship. How well do we live up to it?

Truly we reap what we sow (Galatians 6:7-8). If we do wrong, we face the consequences. The Bible understands that there is no easy equation, no *quid pro quo,* between morality and consequences. Job suffered greatly though he was righteous, and Peter realized that his denial of Christ only brought him more love from Christ rather than a penalty of some sort. Yet our actions (both good and bad) have consequences of some sort; and many times in our lives we stumble, we sin. Some fall into serious sin. Therefore, says Paul, if someone "is detected in a transgression," those who are Spirit-filled should help that person be restored "in a spirit of gentleness" (Galatians 6:1), taking care that temptation does not come their way, too.

Imagine what kind of Christian fellowship that situation would entail. Think about a covenantal group in which all offer and look forward to mutual support and accountability. If someone sins, he or she will not be gossiped about or harshly shamed or excluded. Instead, the person will be helped, guided, and restored by friends. Those friends, in turn, will know their own hearts well enough to know that they, too, have weaknesses that Satan could exploit. They are not conceited; they do not selfishly compare themselves more favorably to others, nor do they denigrate themselves in self-hating comparison to other people (Galatians 5:26; 6:3).

That kind of Christian fellowship presupposes love, compassion, mutual (never one-way) accountability, and patience. That kind of Christian ministers to others where they all are, not where we think they should be! There is no self-righteous control, one-way accountability, "passive aggressive" behavior, envy, strife, and so forth. There is instead the Spirit who empowers and guides and forgives and leads.

The Christian teachers are particularly blessed as those who guide and instruct. Thus Paul advises the Galatians to share generously with their teachers (Galatians 6:6).

Christians should "bear one another's burdens" (Galatians 6:2), yet each person must bear his or her own loads (Galatians 6:5). This seems to be a contradiction. But verse 2 refers to the mutuality and helpfulness that Christians, led by the Spirit, show to other people. We are eager and willing to help other people with whatever burdens they face. Yet one must not neglect one's own burdens. That is, Christians are not called to drop everything and, in effect, become enslaved to other people's needs and burdens. Each Christian has personal burdens and a personal walk with Christ with which he or she must be engaged. The Christian life can be led in a healthy manner only as one takes personal stock of one's discipleship, gifts, and spiritual fruit; thus verse 5.

The term *burn-out* is very common these days. Some of our burn-out comes because we overly extend our time or succumb to pressure to serve (instead of serving from the heart) or become discouraged. This, too, is a matter of carrying our own load. We need to know ourselves and our time commitments well enough that we do not fall into serious burn-out. In Paul's time the problem was not burn-out but outright persecution and sometimes death. Thus he exhorts his Galatian friends not to give up and says, "Let us not grow weary in doing what is right," for the Lord knows our hearts and rewards us (Galatians 6:9-10).

LIBERTY TOGETHER

• Read Galatians 6:1-10. On a chalkboard or large piece of paper, list qualities of Christian fellowship. What kinds of qualities does one need to be a true Christian friend?

• Have you ever been in a covenant group of any kind that offered serious accountability and support for "the state of your soul"? If so, what was it like? Did it, or do you think it could, help you mature in your faith? Is this something you yearn for or would be willing to try? Explain.

• How do you and other members of your community of faith bear one another's burdens? How important is that to you? Are you willing to reveal your burdens in order to have someone else help you bear them? What does it mean to you to cast your cares on the Lord, or on a human representative?

• Have you ever felt "burned out" at your church? What was the reason? Did it have to do with you (your attitudes or your time commitments) or with other factors? How do we avoid burn-out?

• Who were your best teachers? What were their qualities? Do particular church school teachers stand out in your mind?

Concluding Words
Read Galatians 6:11-18

Paul made a notation in his own handwriting. He was not dictating the letter to his secretary at this point, as he apparently often did (see, for example, 1 Corinthians 16:21; 2 Thessalonians 3:17). A scribe would have written more neatly; and if Paul had eye problems (as suggested above), his handwriting might have been large (Galatians 6:11). But he wrote his own words to say, once again, that circumcision does not matter for the Galatians. The gift of the Holy Spirit that makes all things new is everything to them (Galatians 6:15).

The teachers of circumcision aimed to make a good showing. In what seems a slightly risqué but perfectly clear simile, Paul says that these teachers could point to their own circumcised genitals to prove they were holy. They did not have the Galatians' best interests in mind; they merely wished to boast about having gained converts to their way of thinking (6:13)!

Paul here takes one final stab at his argument against the necessity of circumcision for the Galatians. From the Judaizers' point of view, there were good reasons to do it. Most of the opposition to Gentile Christian mission efforts came from the Jews. Being circumcised could have a dual protective benefit: providing an unmistakable sign of Judaism and inclusion in the covenant and freedom from the persecution of Rome, which was generally tolerant of Jews. In addition, as has already been mentioned, they felt they could gain a few points with God by gaining converts who would strictly adhere to the letter and ritual of the Law.

However, as Paul continually countered, those who most advocated circumcision and the law found great difficultly in keeping the whole law themselves. Nevertheless, they were eager for new Galatian "trophies," new adherents to their own legalistic cadre. Converting the Galatians to their way of thinking mattered most to these teachers, not the soundness of their doctrine or the well-being of the church.

Calvin Roetzel also comments, "It is possible that Paul intends to draw an unfavorable comparison between the 'good showing in the flesh' (i.e., circumcision) of his addressees and the 'marks' of Jesus (scars) that have been inflicted on his body by beatings, shipwreck, and other causes."[5] Paul had the scars to prove his sincerity and authority! Paul's scars came to him through his discipleship, while the scar of circumcision was the first step toward being enslaved to a salvation through works—which was no salvation (Galatians 6:7-9).

And so Paul declared, in effect, "Back off" (Galatians 6:17). Paul's own circumcision mattered less than his physical traumas that were signs of his sufferings for Jesus' sake (Acts 9:15-16). But a blunt dismissal was not his last word. As we have seen elsewhere in his letter, his harsh words are later moderated; his ultimate goal was not so much to scold as to restore the former cordial relationship he and the Galatian congregations had experienced. Thus Paul invoked God's peace both for the Galatians and for Israel itself, that is, for both the uncircumcised and the circumcised (Galatians 6:16), and concluded with a word of blessing by Jesus for his brothers and sisters (Galatians 6:18).

CONCLUDING WORDS

• Letter writing is becoming a lost art. Nevertheless, discuss ways in which you might be a Christian servant to someone via e-mail or "snail mail." Who might appreciate a card or letter or message? With whom have you dropped out of touch?

• Read Galatians 6:11-18. Review again Paul's argument to the Galatians. What are the values and detriments of listening to "those who want to make a good showing"? What do they hope to accomplish? What does Paul suggest as a better way?

• Now try to summarize the major themes of the entire letter to the Galatians. How do you now understand the meaning and importance of the law in this context? of freedom in Christ? of equality and liberty?

IN CLOSING

• What for you are the most important insights from your study? What impact have these insights had on your faith? on how you understand and relate to God through Jesus Christ? Is there any sense in which you will feel that you are a new creation as a result of your reflection on this Scripture? How would you describe that?

• Close with prayer for all those who are kept in bondage to inappropriate or unhealthy rules and ritual and for the liberation that new life in Christ will bring.

---

[1] From "Narrative Hunger and Silent Witness: An Interview With Reynolds Price," by Susan Ketchin, in *The Georgia Review*, Fall, 1993; pages 531–532.

[2] From "Narrative Hunger and Silent Witness: An Interview With Reynolds Price"; pages 531–532.

[3] From *Galatians*, by Hans Dieter Betz (Fortress Press, 1979); page 33.

[4] From *The Letters of Paul*, by Calvin J. Roetzel (Westminster John Knox Press, 1998); pages 59–60.

[5] From *The Letters of Paul*; page 63.